ALL Set TO GO PLACES AND DO THINGS!

I am spending the night at UNCLE JOE'S TOURIST CAMP, at Dalton, Ga., on Rte. 41-3, where I find free garages and all modern conveniences. Prices reasonable. I wish you were here now.

Dad & Mother

GAS, FOOD, AND LODGING

BY JOHN BAEDER

ABBEVILLE PRESS · PUBLISHERS · NEW YORK

For Jane

Editor: Walton Rawls

Library of Congress Cataloging in Publication Data:
Baeder, John
  Gas, food, and lodging.
  1. United States—Social life and customs—20th
century—Pictorial works. 2. United States—Description
and travel—Views. 3. Postal cards—United States.
I. Title
El69.B25   973   81-5427
ISBN 0-89659-322-3 (paper) AACR2

Picture Credits

For kind permission to reproduce postcards from their
collections, the author wishes to thank the following
friends: Andy Brown, p. 19 upper left, lower left, upper
right; p. 27; p. 63 upper right; p. 83 center. Dave
Freund, p. 31. Dorothy Globus, p. 10; p. 45 lower.
Richard Gutman, p. 19 lower right. Wayne Harvey, p. 15.
Jim Heimann, p. 25 upper left; p. 27; p. 63 upper right.
Kenneth Kneitel, p. 2 upper; p. 4; p. 8; p. 100. Paul
Kreyling, p. 19 upper left; p. 41 upper right. Newly
(West) and Don Preziosi, p. 37; p. 43 lower left; p. 60.
Charles Smith, p. 2 lower; p. 43 upper right; Ken
Weinstein, p. 97 lower. John West, p. 18; p. 44 lower
right; p. 85; p. 103 lower left. Gary Wright, p. 37 upper
left; p. 61; p. 92 upper right.

Contents

Acknowledgments

The Kelly-Springfield Good Roads Special, which is touring the country in the interests of good roads.

We are all on a journey—we have our own personal odysseys that continue every moment of the day. *Gas, Food, and Lodging* is just one of mine. The path is not taken alone. It is shared by many—some directly, some indirectly. Everyone shares and contributes to one's quest, and one's craft, and one's life. I thank all those I know for where I am, and especially those people who supplied me with postcards that one day would influence me to change my entire life.

There are a special few that have provided an energy that directly affected this book: my art dealer, Ivan Karp, who first looked at four "postcard" paintings, and with his vision and foresight saw more than I did. He and John Kacere were pivotal figures in my painting career; Julie Bresciani, whose encouragement and support have given me a new outlook on myself and my art; Sara Jane Freymann, Steven Schwartz, and Steven Heller, who provided thrust in the early days with the manuscript and design.

And I am grateful to all the delightful people on my odyssey to postcard images. Their warmth and enthusiasm have continued to overwhelm me, and the many friends and kindred spirits who shared common sensibilities and passions and provided me with additional images that contributed to the book: Andy Brown, Ken Brown, Dave Freund, Dorothy Globus, Jim Heimann, Wayne Harvey, Richard Johnson, Ken Kneitel, Paul Kreyling, Newly (West) and Don Preziosi, Leah Schnall, Charles R. Smith, Ken Speiser, Ken Weinstein, John West, and Gary Wright.

Special thanks to Mathew Spinello, who has supplied me with cards through the years. I only know Mathew through letters, but he knows my tastes inside-out, and he has been a valuable asset in shaping my collection; my editor Walton Rawls, for his initial boost with the odyssey idea; Peggy Tagliarino for her appreciation and concern.

Praise to Jane Braddock, my partner and other self, for all her patience, insight, and magic.

Foreword

When we first learned about *Gas, Food, and Lodging*, it occurred to us that sooner or later we would be asked to write an introduction. It seemed a perfect marriage of minds—John Baeder and us—as mutually flattering as the union of Prince Charles and Lady Di, or at least Lucy and Ricky.

After all, we share with John a passion for the American roadside. We are as exhilarated as he is by the silver curves of a diner as sleek as Mercury's winged helmet, or the lingo of an old Navy cook who slides us a "cup of mud" to accompany a breakfast of "Adam and Eve on a raft." John Baeder is the only man we know who can wax eloquent over a dish of tapioca pudding at Mom's Cafe.

After all these things we had shared with John, how could anyone else introduce *Gas, Food, and Lodging*?

But a funny thing happened on the way to the typewriter. We sat down one day to chronicle all the great highway adventures we had with him, hoping to choose the best of them as an introduction to this book . . . and we came up dry. We realized that the thousands of miles we had traveled with John all happened on our living room couch, with a copy of his previous book *Diners* in our hands. Our farflung friendship with this remarkable artist had never broken the boundaries of home.

The vicarious travels were augmented by the half-dozen times John came to visit us, always on his way to or from a place he was tracking down for *Gas, Food, and Lodging*. From his jacket pocket he'd produce old postcards and photographs of funky roadside cafes and ridiculously named motels. From the back of his car came his own beautiful etchings and silkscreens and vintage gas station magazines.

Over Sunday chicken dinners (with the mashed potatoes holding their own little crater of gravy), John regaled us in his soft Dixie accent with stories of the places he had been and the people he had met. And we matched him with our own tales of adventure while writing *Trucker* and *Roadfood*. Many hours later, John would be off again, and we waved as he cut through the night heading back to the highway.

Our old traveling companion John Baeder is a master of armchair magic. To read his words is to fall effortlessly under his spell. No other chronicler of the American roadside has evoked the glory of diners the way his first book did. Now *Gas, Food, and Lodging* expands his vision to more of highway's culture and, backwards in time, to memory.

Postcards are collectible investments, but to John Baeder they are charms. Their frozen images and even the messages on the back are an enchanted access route into the past. *Gas, Food, and Lodging* is a book about how people and places change, and how they don't. Guided by his own and other people's memories, John travels a fantastic landscape of Ditty Wah Ditty Motels, Dutch Diners, and Wigwam Villages. It is a sensory journey, perfumed by cafe griddles or musty motel rooms colored flamingo pink and decorated with chenille bedspreads.

You can hear in the way he writes that John Baeder is spellbound, that he falls so hard in love with the postcard images that he wants to devour them with his eyes. He is a hopeless romantic, seduced by the road's calling; and he is enough of an artist to seduce us.

What we are trying to say is that this book has a soul, a story-telling artist's soul. After reading the manuscript of *Gas, Food, and Lodging*, the first thing we did was get in our car and drive. It didn't matter where. We spun the odometer going to favorite places we hadn't been to in a while, just to make sure they were still there . . . Weenieville, Clam Castle, the Injun Trading Post up the road. We renewed our friendship with old haunts and snatched up handfuls of postcards on the way home. "Wish you were here," we wrote to friends, who doubtless shrugged their shoulders when they got the cards we had written at our dining room table at home. But it wasn't Weenieville or Injun Village we were thinking about when we wrote the cards. It was *Gas, Food, and Lodging*, a magical place to be.

JANE AND MICHAEL STERN
WILTON, CONNECTICUT

A brief introduction

This is a not a book *of* postcards, or *about* postcards. This is a book about feelings, and the feelings that are evoked by postcard images—images that are a distillation of our culture; a reflection of our society; and a document of the growth of the great American roadside.

Books of and about postcards abound: books that vary in style, format, taste, and price—from the whimsical to the scholarly. Various authors and specialists in the hobby and profession have dealt with the topics of postcard publishers, artists, and photographers, and worldwide, domestic, and local postcard histories. They are all lively, worthwhile, and fun to read and look at. I recommend them to anyone with the slightest interest in postcards and the craze they've recently created.

Postcards and their images played a pivotal part in my life. They were a catalyst in setting thoughts and feelings in motion. Postcards were responsible for a career change and a new beginning. They provided a source of energy and a rebirth. I felt the need to return to my source of inspiration, to pay homage, to re-live some fantasies, and to turn them into realities.

John Baeder
May, 1982

9

The Big Duck, Riverhead, Long Island. N. Y.

How I got into postcards, and how they got into me.

I have a classic Capricornian calling: back to the earth. It's respecting and doing something about that in your life—basics of the food, clothing, and shelter variety. Gas, food, and lodging are embodied in these basics. It's simple—food for your automobile and food for your body. The automobile is an extension of your body, and your body is an extension of your soul. It's the full-circle concept.

And, I love basic ideas—like reduction and miniaturization; time frozen in space, and space frozen in time. We are bombarded with this concept every day, from the moment we pick up the morning paper to the moment we turn off the tube. This idea promotes and creates new feelings for a visual image that is captured in this space–time framework. An image is re-focused; the scale affects the senses, and our consciousness becomes altered. And this is what art is all about: the visual event becomes a larger-than-life experience. Postcard images involving gas, food, and lodging do this for me.

For example, I project myself into the image as if I were actually there. There is an element of fantasy in wishing to go inside the picture of a cafe, for instance, and to sit at the counter and look at the surroundings and feel the environment, smell the odors, and listen to the tapestry of sounds.

All of us are voyeurs at heart, and perhaps this attitude of behavior is my own brand of voyeurism. During my travels, I sometimes enter a new town that's been untainted by present-day touches of plastic signs, rehabilitation, and the usual phony-decor that marks our commercial strips; I will drive down the street and feel as though I were passing into a postcard image stuck in time–space. (This is a rare event, but such towns do exist.)

And then the process happens in reverse. An intense curiosity propels me to want more images from the postcard, so I may travel into the card, and wander around as if nobody were there. Perhaps it's primal in the sense that there is a history of darkness in the making and experiencing of images. In ancient caves, images of matchless power were painted on walls and ceilings, settings much like the boxes (caves) that are the home for my post-cards of gas, food, and lodging images. Man has a faculty for image-making that is matched to his need for images. As an artist, this is why I focus on this concept with the postcards.

I am a painter, and like all of us wrapped-up in the visual world, pictures were just as important as Pablum as an early means of feeding and nourishment. When I was a kid growing up in Atlanta, Georgia, I had a tremendous need for magazines and the pictures they contained. I couldn't get enough of them, and I needed constant refilling. I was visually overweight. My parents told me I was a picky eater, and now I am aware that I was also fairly discriminating in my choice of visual material, too. However, I had to sample everything—which was not true of the food that was put in front of me.

My parents subscribed to all the major magazines, and my happiest moments were greeting the mail after school and waiting for the mailman on that special day, Saturday. Soon the household magazines weren't enough, and I had to subscribe to my own variety. I had to have magazines that had something to do with transportation—airplanes, automobiles, and trains. I wasn't scientific or mechanical by nature, but I had a love affair with pictures of things that moved.

Soon I was introduced to old magazines. I liked them because of the change in time that was evident in the pictures. Many of these magazines were discovered from grammar school paper sales. I'd always hang around until all the donated bundles were delivered, and then I had the thrill of untying the stacks and pulling out magazines that interested me. Many were early issues that had been nesting in garages, attics, and basements. They had a musty odor that was intense and personal for me. Like perfume. These magazines were my first dose of the past, and, as with the postcards, the feelings were erotic in nature. Of course at ten years old I didn't know exactly what that was, but I knew it felt good. Reluctantly I would return to class, late of course, and my teacher would send me back to the sidewalk to return the magazines. She didn't understand my plight—my intense need to be fed these magazines, with their little pictures that smelled so good. The big stake trucks were collecting all these treasures. It made me sad. I had to keep the magazines, so I hid them under some bushes and waited until school cleared out and returned to the nest for my food.

I'd go home and sit in my grandmother's favorite chair. It was also my favorite chair—covered in a large floral print, and, oh, so soft and comfortable. It was next to a window, and I could feel the late spring breezes caress this newfound sensory experience. I'd feast on these magazines and smell the residue of grandma and the must from the magazines' age. Then I'd treat myself to a giant bowl of tapioca pudding, and consume. Picture after picture.

The industrial revolution paved the way for one of the most phenomenal events in American history: the invention of the automobile. Through the pioneering spirit and the restlessness of the American character, the great American roadside was created.

I feel close to this spirit—expecting the unexpected, close to the restlessness and the need for change; close to the road and the want for the unknown.

When I started to collect postcards, gas stations, eateries, tourist cabins, and motels caught my eye most quickly. I felt a direct relationship and connection with these subjects. They fed off one another. I collected other images that aroused my heart and eyeballs, but there was a reason for the "roadside" material. On an unconscious level, I perceived it was because as a child I didn't have the opportunity to travel by auto and to experience road culture—and this was in the forties, during the final epoch of roadside goodness.

Allen Wright, Jr., was the first honest-to-goodness postcard dealer I met. He and his father had a booth at a major antique show in New York City. This was in the late sixties—the hippie movement and the Viet Nam war were in full swing, and I was getting into postcards. Once in a while I'd see a box or two at antique shops or flea markets; I was ignorant of their growing popularity. It was startling to come upon a booth of nothing but postcards. (OK, a few stamps. . . .) I was interested in gas, food, and lodging-type cards; however, I was also purchasing other subjects that astounded my eyes. Allen grasped my interests and invited me to his office; he had more cards filed away.

I subwayed quickly down to the lower depths of Manhattan, in the Wall Street area, where hidden on the fifth floor of an old building on Nassau Street was his office. Allen and his father sat deeply entrenched in postcards. They were all over the place, well kept and serious. Allen knew what I wanted and pulled out a drawer. I started to bathe in pictures—images that made me weep with joy. I was beginning to become involved more with the linen-finish card, and Allen had thousands of them.

Returning to my office after a "lunch-afternoon," I was preoccupied and drained with visual awakenings. My co-workers looked at me and asked if I were ill. I was, and answered with intoxicated slurs that I had postcarditis. Days went by and I re-examined the cards and felt literally inebriated. I would get a tingle and that was the signal —another postcard fix. That seemed to be the only cure, so I would call Allen for an appointment and hop downtown to purchase heaps of cards. I was hooked.

Allen invited me to join the local postcard club, which I did, with reluctance because I am not a joiner of clubs. They never interested me, too much blah-blah. But the postcard club did offer monthly meetings where dealers gathered to sell their wares. Then there was the yearly bash of dealers from the surrounding area. My first time at one of these events was overwhelming; I had never seen so many postcards and postcard "nuts" in my life. My eyes got sore along with my thumbs.

By now I had become thoroughly addicted and started to place ads in various antiques newspapers that catered to the trade and to collectors. I would specifically request cards for gas, food, and lodging-related subjects. The variety of cards I received was downright ludicrous. People were hot to sell anything—flowers and cats and little rosy-cheeked girls watering more flowers. There was good merchandise amongst all the froufrou, and the more sophisticated dealers would understand my "wants" but couldn't quite grasp the "whys," because at that time there was no value in my specialized categories.

The ads had to be discontinued because the responses were too frequent, and I couldn't keep up with all of them. Yes, it was great to get a surprise package in the mailbox everyday, but after a while that began to wear off; it was too much trouble returning the cards and writing polite letters. In fact, I stopped (officially) collecting postcards for a while; I felt full and overweight.

Allen Wright told me I created a fad with the gas, food, and lodging category. He said, "People are coming up to me [at postcard meets] and asking for diners, and motels, and gas stations. . . . They never used to do that. . . . You really did something with your paintings, and your book!" I happily acknowledged Allen's comments. Yes, there are a lot of people asking for these cards illustrating the American roadside. I have noticed that some dealers have a separate "Diner" selection, and "American Roadside" section. Times have changed and collecting habits have, too. I personally feel the Bicentennial had an effect on this re-awakening, and I am proud I was involved with it. There is a new breed, the "me-too" crowd;

they are younger and more influenced by the media and other collectors, than followers of an inner sense and inner vision. That's part of the change, and it's good for the dealers because they take advantage and mark up prices to astronomical highs. It's bad for the serious collectors who have worked hard acquiring cards and are victimized by a superficial market.

DUANESBURG, N.Y.

PLEASANT VIEW RESTAURANT AND DRIVE-IN SNACK BAR
ROUTE 3 -- TWIN MOUNTAIN, N. H.   D527

Royal Park Court - 25 Miles South Of Savannah On U.S.17 - Richmond Hill, Ga.

2-S-38

CAFE AT TAYLOR'S COURT   ON HY. 5 AND 80   GAINESVILLE, MO.

AT DICK WICK HALL'S FAMOUS LAUGHING GAS STATION.

THIS IS THE LAUGHING GAS STATION

WHERE WE SELL GASOLINE % ILE AND TAKE YOUR MONEY WITH A SMILE —
OLD ROKEFELLER MADE HIS PILE — AND MAYBE WE WILL — AFTERWHILE
WE ARE HERE TO FILL YOUR TANK AND GET YOUR MONEY IN OUR BANK —
SO STOP AND SEE US AS YOU PASS — FILL YOUR TANK WITH LAUGHING GAS
YOU DON'T HAVE TO CROSS THE TRACK WHEN YOU WANT TO SPEND YOUR JACK —
DRIVE RIGHT UP WITH YOUR OLD BUS AND LEAVE YOUR MONEY HERE WITH US
YOU WILL GET YOUR DOLLAR'S WORTH IN GASOLINE OR ELSE IN MIRTH
WE WILL TRADE YOU ANYTHING — MINING STOCK FOR A DIAMOND RING —

FIFTEEN ACRES OF SAGE BRUSH LAND FOR AN OLD CALLIOPE — SECONDHAND —
FIVE NEW TIRES WE WANT TO SELL — CANNED TOMOATOES AND BLACKBERRY JELL —
ICE CREAM, SODA AND ALMOST BEER — ACETYLENE WELDING DONE RIGHT HERE —
SALOME WATER — PAINTED JOKES — WILD GOAT GLANDS — GOOD BYE FOLKS.

SALOME, ARIZONA
"Where She Danced"
Send a Postal to the Folks—They might like to hear the Jolks.

15

IOWA'S MOST BEAUTIFUL FILLING STATION AND THE FACES YOU WILL MEET AT CRESTON, IOWA.

SHERIDAN OIL COMPANY.

The photo and "linen" postcards, and how they changed my life.

There are two distinct postcard "styles" I enjoy. The "style" stems from the method of reproduction. One is the photographic card, and the other is the "linen-finish" card. Both cards are totally unique and seem at opposite poles from each other.

The photographic card, better known as the photocard or—in the trade—the "black and white," is highly sought after, and by far the most collectible. For obvious reasons—it's a photograph. Not only postcard nuts, but photographers, designers, historians, architects, actors, musicians, and general collectors are clamoring for photocards. Why? They are miniscule, scarce historical documents, and they are getting less available. The old law of supply and demand has made the photocard market go out of whack. Prices are obnoxious. Lately, the photograph has become "collectible" and valuable in the so-called "investment" circles. And the photocard follows. Its reduced scale makes no difference in terms of value; its scarcity does. And there are more varieties of images in photocards than normally seen in the photo-collecting trade per se.

My photocards are in the gas, food, and lodging area. (I may go off the road once in a while; when other images pop up that I like, I'll buy.) They are rare and difficult to locate, unless one is a dealer and constantly on the prowl, with "feelers" out every minute of the day and an absolute obsessive–compulsive need for cards to keep, or re-sell. So, as a collector, I have to pay the price, which is getting higher day by day. In fact, some prices are downright ridiculous; dealers play with "limits" and see how far they can go with collectors—and other dealers.

Photocards offer a lot to my visual fantasy life, which consists of an "I-wish-I-were-there-then" attitude. I take the spy glass (the Agfa 8x is the most comfortable) and travel across an image. I may start with a doorway and move over to a window, pull back, like on a camera dolly, and travel down the street and back again, returning to a few signs, some people, and a couple of cars. I get a glimpse of everything. Up, and around. Down, and across. Smooth and careful viewing. Visual caresses.

HOTEL PINECREST
AT LAKE STRAWBERRY, CALIFORNIA

HOTEL PINECREST AT LAKE STRAWBERRY, TUOLUMNE CO., CALIFORNIA

Stuckey's Candy Shoppe - Junction U.S. 15 and 301 - Summerton, S.C.

THE MINERS HAT
SANDWICHES — FOUNTAIN SERVICE
CAR SERVICE
EAST CITY LIMITS   KELLOG, IDAHO

30965

THE BIG RED APPLE   123000

"THE WIGWAM"
2 MILES FROM ADRIAN, MICH. ON U.S. 127

"Only Petrified Wood Filling Station in the World"
W. G. Brown, Builder and Owner   Lamar, Colo.

103

19

ROYAL CAFE AND DRIVE-IN — On Highway 90 — DEL RIO, TEXAS

Intersection Highways to San Antonio, El Paso, Laredo, and Mexico

Local, itinerant, and souvenir-company employed photographers were responsible for the majority of photo-cards I particularly enjoy. Regardless of their "status" as photographers, I call them "street" photographers simply because they set up their cameras on the street, aimed the lens—bang, poof—and a picture of everlasting beauty came from this act. These photographers (or artists, as I'd like to call them) didn't have intense, sophisticated training. Or a literary sense. They did have an unconscious sense of design and an incisive eye that could perceive an image with clarity, and integrity, and honesty. And that's what photocards are all about: honesty and reality. Out and open; it's all there.

Not so with the linen-finish cards, which is the reason I am drawn to them. They function on the other side of reality. They aren't open, and they aren't all there. They are pure fantasy. Visual entertainment. They are like a bowl of Jell-O—not much there, but it *does* make you feel good.

When I was a kid in the forties, the linen card was in its heyday. I was repelled by them, because they were so outrageous, so "messed-with," so unrealistic-looking for my sensitive green eyes. I felt cheated; how dare those postcard printing people fool *me*!

It wasn't their fault. The American printers didn't have the expertise. Germany had it, and we didn't care for Germany during the thirties and forties. Ironically, the leading manufacturer of linen cards in the country was a German, by the name of Curt Teich, in Chicago, Illinois. Linen cards were manufactured for one primary reason: inexpensive color reproduction. Photocards became expensive because of the photo paper, and the monochromatic tone wasn't "romantic" enough for the traveling tourist who wished to spice up a trip with an inexpensive souvenir that was fun and lively looking, and above all—colorful.

The linen card is basically the merger of a photocard and art, but it has gone through shock treatment. For instance, at Curt Teich, there were eight or nine photo-retouchers (all men) who would take their little airbrushes and remove unwanted shadows, telephone poles and wires, adjoining buildings, automobiles, or other obtrusive objects that got in the way of the "advertised" product.

These "forgotten-little-folk-artists," as I like to call them, "blew" in a fresh new sky, or new cloud wisps, or a sunset at "high-noon" light, turned daylight into nightlight. They would remove or install trees and shrubs, cars and people (see the "Monteagle Diner"), silhouette, shade, lighten, darken. If customers didn't know what they wanted, Teich would do what *he* wanted, always adding or subtracting—like adding "graphics" for visual effect, outlining to define areas; snapping up the focus when there wasn't any; romanticizing when there was no romance. Images were overlapped, joined, butted, and packed into tiny spaces so the viewers could feel they were getting more for less.

Teich ran a tough ship. He printed millions of cards a week. Women were segregated on a separate floor. They did all the color work, painting on glass the flat colors linen cards are so known for. Red. Yellow. Blue. Black. (Teich was proud they used two blues, for a better "effect.") All day long they sat, with Teich standing over their shoulders—as he did with the retouchers—repainting the little images. I'd give anything to have watched them. Re-creating realities. Making postcard history they would never know about.

There was no smoking, no coffee breaks, one bathroom break (eeek!), no talking, and there were time limits on finishing a card. One image usually was done in eight hours. A postcard sweatshop—no wonder so many linen-type cards were produced in a thirty-year period.

I theorized that the linen paper was used to make the finished image look more like a "painting." Why not? With all the retouching and little frilly hand-coloring, it literally became a painting. The linen texture provided the viewer with an illusion. The images were idealized anyway, so why not go a step further with the textured paper? Not so. In the late twenties Teich brought over a new printing press from Germany; it printed better on the textured linen-finish paper. On the earlier "white-border" cards, the ink took longer to dry, and they absorbed the ink because the paper was slicker. (By the way, these cards are great to bathe in for visual enjoyment. They are flat and posterlike in appearance and reminiscent of early color lithographs.)

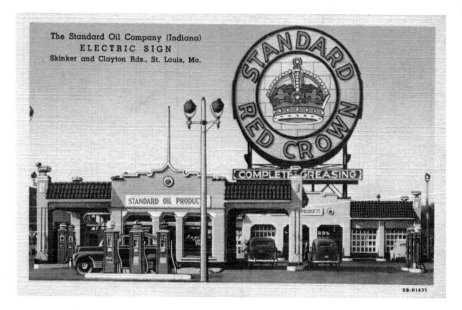

THE TAVERN, EAGLE BAY, N.Y.

BEE HIVE LUNCH ROOM, HAYNESVILLE, VT. 42.

ELK CITY, OKLA.
QUEEN OF THE WEST

FLORIDA MOTOR LINE, MUSA ISLE INDIAN VILLAGE

JOYCE'S CANDY SHOP IS LOCATED ⅓ MILE FROM BAY ST. LOUIS
BRIDGE. WE SPECIALIZE IN OUR DELICIOUS CREAMY PRALINES AND
FOR OUR PAPER SHELL PECANS - ON HIGHWAY U.S. 90

LAWRENCE TOURIST CABINS. CHESTER. N. Y.   TEL. CHESTER 15

FROM THE WEST—U.S. ROUTE 6.   FROM N.Y.C.—ROUTE 2 and 17.   E-4275

DUFFY'S *Streamliner*

Federal Made in U.S.A.
FEDERAL MATCH CORP. NEW YORK

ROUTE 20   WORLD'S   GREATEST
NORTH OXFORD, MASS.

CLOSE COVER BEFORE STRIKING

WHERE QUALITY REIGNS   JIMMIE EVANS FLYER   TEL 2-8043

NEVER CLOSED

FEDERAL MATCH CORP NEW YORK

CLOSE COVER BEFORE STRIKING

PLEASANT ST.   ROUTE 6 NEW BEDFORD, MASS.

BAR

CHARCOAL BROILED STEAKS

PORT SILVER DINER

FOUNTAIN - DRIVE-IN CANTEEN   PATIO

COFFEE SHOP - DINING ROOMS

AIRWAY DINER

THE DINER

COFFEE SHOP

CORNER PACIFIC HIGHWAY AND LAUREL ST., SAN DIEGO, CALIF.

Super Chief Diner, Highway 395, Carson City, Nevada

OPEN
SUPER CHIEF

SERVING Breakfast Lunch Dinner
PAN FRIED CHICKEN

DINER
VIRGINIA & TRUCKEE

BREAKFAST

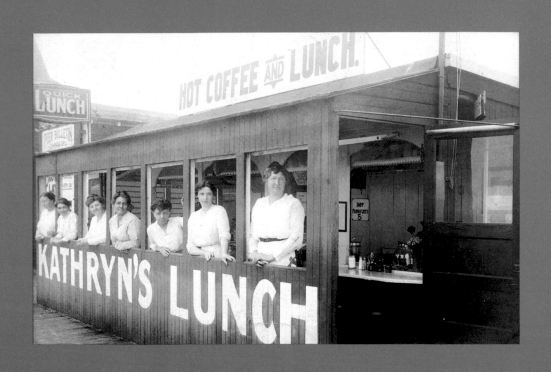

LOWER DELLS FILLING STATION, WISCONSIN DELLS, WIS.

PA 115—The Turnpike's Picturesque Midway Inn and Service Station at Bedford
"America's Dream Highway"

ROARIN' ROHRER

OKLAHOMA'S MOST BEAUTIFUL STATION
ON U. S. 270, McALESTER, OKLA.
STREAM LINED SERVICE

56892

Edgerly Lunch Room

NIPMUC QUICK LUNCH

SMOKE TEMPLE 5¢ STRAIGHT REALLY WORTH THE

SMOKE CLASS A 10¢ CIGAR

CAMP ALOHA
Mich — 7

Hires

THE ENTRANCE
PROFIT

BALLENGER'S PARK – MONTEZUMA OHIO

Twenty years go by, and linen cards enter postcard history. Taking a new look at their visual properties, I collect as many as possible in my interest group that appeal to me. As I study and investigate them, with the Agfa glass again, the heightened visual unreality becomes *a* reality. I reflect and reject all my younger values. These cards are giving me delight, and I immerse myself in this newfound enchantment, awe, and above all—inspiration.

These cards have become an extension of my vision (along with the photocard), but this was a new vision, and a new appreciation that made it exciting. The "new" isn't easy to accept so soon. I took my time and let it sink in. After all, a vision made up of unreality and a surreal look at this new world around me—gas, food, and lodging—was scary. Something was churning inside as a result of this enlightenment. I saw the cards as paintings, and I saw them as paintings that I might be part of. I had an intense desire to see these images on a larger scale. My viewing glass gave me this perception and new vision. I still traveled in the same manner as I did with the photocard, but it was a different kind of travel. It was a "yellow-brick-road" kind of travel, and it was a new look at my inner self. I knew they were *art*. (And they could become a higher art.)

I said to myself, "Why don't you paint these images if you feel so strongly?" I hesitated. I was afraid. It was too overwhelming. (Love *can* be overwhelming.) I had the usual excuses: Will I be a success? Will I be a failure? I don't have enough time. It'll take too long. The basic excuses of fear. I was patient and listened to the fear. I listened: "Anything can happen, if you let it." Ah, that was good. And I listened again, "Branches break; the tree is whole." Ah, that was comforting, too. I wanted to dig up some more self-respect. We all can use more every once in a while. I wanted to use more inner strengths. And to *use* is to *gain*. So, I said good-bye to twelve years of advertising and hello to the unknown world of becoming a painter. The first paintings were 42 x 66″ versions of 3½ x 5½″ postcards. There were diners, gas stations, tourist courts, motels, and small-town street scenes. And this is why *Gas, Food, and Lodging* is a way of paying homage, of returning, to my inspiration, and of working out many feelings that were catalytic in my rebirth as a person and an artist.

I look at these early "linen" postcard paintings, and they still hold up. Some are stronger than others. They were a phase, a beginning moment, a boost for the burner. I moved off the color linen image and on to the black

Pete's Melody, 1972
Acrylic on canvas, 42x66″,
collection Diane and Judd Maze,
New York, New York

and white photo image, using photocards as a base of visual operation. These images were mostly of small towns and corner drugstores and gas stations and other auto-related images. At this time, the photocard pushed me into painting more realistically. I was soon labeled a "photo-realist." I was a few years late, or second generation, as the artworld likes to put it. I was disturbed a bit by the label. I just wanted to be a painter. I didn't use all the mechanical tools, fuzzy backgrounds and extra-sharp foregrounds, slick paint, and I didn't want to have the self-consciousness that gets in the way of many "photo-realist" painters. I just went ahead and painted what I believed in. See my book *Diners* (New York: Harry N. Abrams, Inc., 1978).

The photo postcard and the linen postcard: two of my best friends, and I will cherish them forever.

Kozy Kabin Kamp, 1972
Acrylic on canvas, 42x66″, collection American Telephone and Telegraph,
New York, New York

Holt's Cafe, 1973
Oil on canvas, 42x66″, Private collection, New York, New York

Grand Canyon Trading Post, 1973
Oil on canvas, 30x48″, collection the artist.

Gas, Food, and Lodging

As automobiles began to roll along the new roads the oil industry started to gush. It experienced rapid growth, just as the auto industry had; they paralleled each other. In the early days of the automobile, gasoline was stored in a "red drum" in a room behind the grocery store. The mysterious "red drum" delivered gasoline to the "motorist" by a bucket and funnel.

Later came the portable shack with a portable hand-operated gasoline pump and a drum of oil. Later came the dispensing pump, looking like a glass-topped monolith oozing its way out of the ground. Actually it was conveniently placed at curbside so Mr. or Mrs. or Ms. Motorist could grab some quick gas for a roll on the road. These pumps had underground storage, a *modern* device. Next, why yes, was the drive-in station with a building to shelter the "attendant." Also toilet facilities.

With these improvements, an operator undertook new responsibilities, and, best of all, he made more money by washing and lubricating a customer's car. (We pay for our laziness, remember? . . .) These chores were first done on a driveway, then a concrete slab was installed beside the building, and, later, a wooden elevated runway or grease rack for lubrication was placed adjacent to the wash rack. Then deeper grease pits became common, but menacing. They were a mess because of drained oil, and rubbish, and water that filled the pits. (Is this where the "pits" expression comes from?) Finally, a welcome improvement: the hydraulic lift. Stations became larger to accommodate the increased demand for services. The "Lubritorium" was born. Stations got taller and equipment improved; "stalls" or "bays" were modernized with tile walls and floors (oooh la-la) and sophisticated heating systems and lighting features.

All this progress was internal progress, but externally these "filling" stations looked dreadful to the eye. Why? Most oil companies had engineering departments

MOOSE MOUNTAIN FILLING STATION,
7½ MILES SOUTH OF SANBORNVILLE, N.H.

with men trained in the design and construction of refineries. (Remember this is the mid-twenties, and stiff, starched collars and tight neckties were the dress of the day—and very stuffy.) The service station was a necessary evil; no special design attention was given to its appearance. Results were architectural tragedy. Engineers *do not* pinch-hit for architects. The tie unloosens.

Oil companies increased their budgets for service station construction and design. Now, they were officially "service" stations, as opposed to "filling" stations. Practically every corner in a community had a service station, and this idea wasn't generally accepted by neighborhoods. Local riff-raff and competition forced the oil companies to give their stations architectural recognition, and architecture departments were created to handle this new area of specialization. Flash. The beginning of oil company color schemes, graphics, and

separate architectural "looks." Gas station styling was upon us. Because of market demand for repairs, tires, batteries, and other automotive accessories, more space was needed for additional sales and display areas.

Occasionally an automotive dealership would join forces with an oil company, and a complete dealership––sales–service unit was established. On the highway, the small independent operator was equally alert and aggressive in developing a higher profit, and he found that his location was ideal for food service. This was efficient for the mom and pop and son and daughter and pet concept. The whole family could pitch in. Living quarters were added, so they could take breaks when business was good, or bad. And, since late tourists and travelers were prospects for sleeping accommodations, the tourist cabin, motel, truckie dorm ideas were added to the station. Gas, Food, and Lodging all under one roof—so cozy.

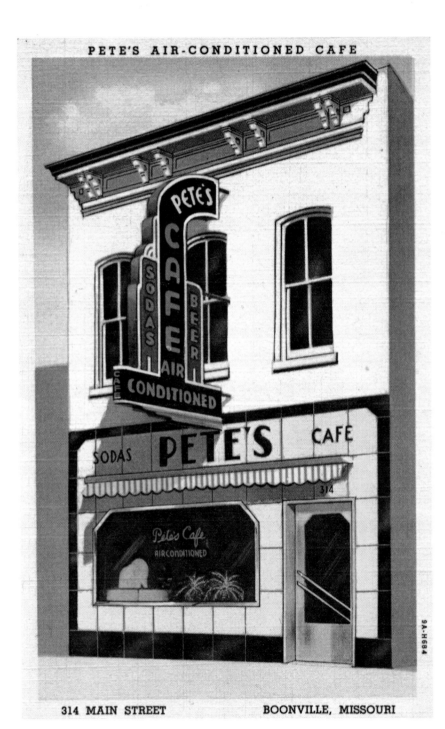

PETE'S AIR-CONDITIONED CAFE

PETE'S CAFE
SODAS
BEER
AIR
CAFE
CONDITIONED

SODAS PETE'S CAFE

314

Pete's Cafe
AIRCONDITIONED

9A-H684

314 MAIN STREET   BOONVILLE, MISSOURI

Court Cafe

DISPENSARY SERVICE   Fresh Fish   Blue Plate Luncheon   Fountain Service   Fresh Oysters

COURT CAFE
On Highways 66 and 85 in the heart of
ALBUQUERQUE, NEW MEXICO
Known from Coast to Coast -- 24 Hour Service
"TOURISTS COME AS YOU ARE"

5A-H610

WESTERN CAFE — ROCK SPRINGS, WYO.

7A-H1948

Branding Iron
Auto Lodge

LARAMIE, WYOMING

MARYVILLE OIL CO.
Big Pump Service Station — Cut Rate
South Edge Maryville, Mo.   Highway 71

Two Stiffs Selling Gas
Lovelock, Nevada

FROM LOVELOCK EAST		FROM LOVELOCK WEST	
Lee Center	14	Hot Springs	41
Mill City	45	Fernley	59
Winnemucca	73	Wadsworth	62
Golconda	89	Sparks	92
Battle Mountain	126	Reno	95
Carlin	178	Truckee	129
Elko	201	Donner Lake	135
Wells	252	Emigrant Gap	159
Wendover	313	Colfax	185
Knolls	352	Auburn	203
Grantsville	404	Sacramento	239
Salt Lake	445	San Francisco	340

Authorized Distributors Of
STANDARD PRODUCTS
ATLAS TIRES and BATTERIES
LUNCHES - DRINKS - ICE CREAM

(OVER)

LATORIA SERVICE STATION
Mannheim Road and Belmont Ave.
Call and see my Family of 22
At home 3337 Ernst St.   Franklin Park, Ill.

10348

Good Hotel, Restaurant, Garage and Tourist Camp Service

At Shady Grove Camp, Valdosta, Ga. On the National Highway.

Adams, Manager Patterson and Devereaux, three Canfield men whom you can depend for proper service for your car.

4 Miles North of Port Henry, N. Y.

69/3

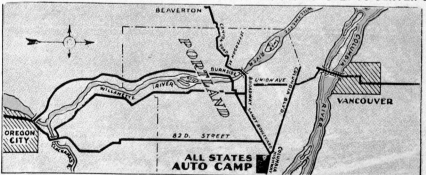

"TUCK IN AT TUCKERS". ALL STATES AUTO CAMP. 15 MINUTES TO CENTER OF CITY.

2710 SANDY BLVD. ON COLUMBIA RIVER HIGHWAY—OPPOSITE INVERNESS GOLF COURSE. 114647

FOLLOW THE SWALLOW TOURIST CAMPS, INC.
SALINA, KANSAS
Convenient as the best Hotel
Comfortable as your own Home
Coffee Shop   Rates $1.50 up   Kiddies play ground

J.C.HARBIN'S TOURIST COTTAGES
MEMPHIS, TENN.

U.S.51 SOUTH

Easy to find

J.C.HARBIN

Fine Food-Beautyrest Mattresses
Swimming Pool-Baths-Steam & Gas Heat

7A-H1821

JACK PINE LODGE
MANISTIQUE,
MICH.

At Sea-View Motor Court,
On the Redwood Highway
3 miles north of Arcata,

PARLOR, BEDROOM AND BATH - KING'S GATEWAY HOTEL - LAND O'LAKES, Wis.   Rice-Maid Photo

Wadhams Service Station — N. 27 St. and W. Wisconsin Ave., Milwaukee, Wisconsin

One of my favorite mottoes in life is: "Expect the unexpected." Or, in simple language: "Ya Never Know...." While driving out west six years ago taking roadside-related photographs for a Smithsonian Bicentennial exhibition, I photographed a sign that simply said: ROADSIDE BUSINESS. It was the usual large, dark-green highway sign with little glass ball reflectors. It affected my thinking and suddenly made me realize it was the title of a book of commercial roadside-relic photographs.

I had, and was getting, marvelous material. I thought about the idea for a while but finally realized it wasn't good enough. It didn't "turn-the-corner." It's easy to take photographs: find a nice old theater, or gas station; raise the camera, click, and presto—a pretty picture. As a painter, I have used photographs as visual notes, and I wanted an idea that had more depth, vision, and passion.

The obvious is always in front of you. Always. We have *all* been in this emotional abyss and re-awakening. I was traveling one of the interstates and passed the seven-hundredth GAS, FOOD, AND LODGING sign: flash, boom— I jumped out of one visual skin and into another. My film idea of traveling the American roadside using the picture postcard all of a sudden moved from twenty-four frames a second to one page per few minutes. I realized that all the film, all the cutting, and all the time didn't appeal to me at the moment. (Ironically it does now, and that project is in the works.) I had accumulated all these wonderful postcards depicting gas, food, and lodging subjects, and they were sitting nestled in my studio doing nothing but pleasing *me*. Why not share them with *others*. A book was a far more productive solution.

Traveling most, or all, of the states, going back to postcard images would have been an ideal journey, and I'm sure I'd pay the price, ending up in a hospital ward for exhaustion. I felt it would be better to concentrate on an accessible area, and I knew that would provide an overview. It is a time-consuming, tiring, but highly addictive activity. Everywhere I went people were endlessly friendly, receptive, and enthusiastic. Displaying old postcard images in front of strangers' faces is quite disarming: they immediately expose an array of feelings and thoughts, and memories.

Many artists and writers practice their own form of odyssey by traveling and relocating to places out of their "norm." It's all part of process and expansion. I temporarily moved to Nashville, Tennessee, from New York City and feel that the new environment has made a huge contribution to my own creative diet, and to this odyssey.

The Odyssey

STOKDALE'S CABINS AT VANTAGE BRIDGE OVER THE COLUMBIA RIVER · WASH.

Monteagle Diner

I entered the "Monteagle Diner," ordered a Barbecue Beef, and approached a couple of waitresses and some locals doing the universally-accepted-most-taken-for-granted drug-trip: coffee and cigarettes. I gave them another kicker by showing them three early "views" of the diner. They were smiling from the cards, and were flipping through the dummy layout of *Gas, Food, and Lodging*—it looked so real they thought it was the actual book. There was some reminiscing about the history of the diner. ("It was a real dining car from a train." "No, it wasn't, it was built chere. . . .") Moments pass and I am left alone talking with Bill Thomas.

Bill is an ex-town policeman and now a contractor. He appreciates postcards and has a loving feeling about them. (Bill is very modest about this.) He has early cards, mostly from the turn of the century, and he refused to admit he was a "collector." Bill owns one *special* card—the one pictured with the "Steinbergian" automobiles and people.

He continued to tell me about the earlier years and all the traffic on old Highway 41, and how the diner gained its reputation because of its location on top of the mountain—a natural stop for travelers. Bill agreed with my point that around 1955–56 was a cut-off period, meaning that the roadside appearance America *knew* was starting its decline at that time. We both didn't articulate this idea; however, we were in perfect accord and understood our own unspoken language. I asked Bill how he felt about this, and he said, "I'm a redneck, I hate to see things change. I'm on the City Council, you know. I'm a City Father . . . but we need changes, and it has to be for the better."

Bill is *no* redneck. He just has a humble sense of himself, and his community, and a deep sense of history.

MONTEAGLE DINER - MONTEAGLE TENN. U.S. 41-64

1949

Bill's Place, Pa.

Driving through the rolling, luscious hills of south-central
Pennsylvania was like riding a winged horse. A definite
"Maxfield Parrish" quality envelops this terrain, and
it was intensified by soft rains. I notice an attractive barn
and antiques store on a downhill curve. Whoa! Pegasus!

I do the normal looking around for a while and find a
couple of goodies, a pair of blue Sunoco gas pump salt and
peppers for a start. Don Williams is coming through in
his mellow fashion on a nearby tapedeck, and I had just
turned him off on my tapedeck. (Yes, Pegasus is equipped
with 8-track.) I find a couple of more good items and
there is a calm. I overhear a Depression-glass story and get

into it—I don't even care about Depression glass. There was a magic developing: her name is Jean Pepples. Jean and her husband run the antiques store and the auction barn upstairs. Not only is Jean a great auction caller, she is also a riot—an extremely vivacious, funny, mouth-a-running, tons-of-smiles-and-winks woman. I really like Jean, and we became instant hits.

Jean approaches me with an iron skillet in her hand. In the skillet are two fried eggs. Immediately I notice they are plastic and are salt and peppers. (One yolk is salt, the other yolk is pepper.) I said to Jean, "How did you know I love, and collect, goofy salt and peppers?" She smiles intuitively, knowing *we* come from the same egg. She tells me there are more crazy salt and peppers and takes me behind the counter to examine two box-loads of S and Ps she just purchased. I go through the boxes and pick out more, wonderful, dumb, S and Ps.

Jean is also an ex-roadside waitress. She still carries a modified beehive-with-bangs. Jean said if it wasn't for her kids, her antiques business, and the auctions, she'd be waitressing. She loves people. She loves to give. She loves to work. It shows all over her.

Jean snaps out an 8 x 10 glossy photo of "Bill's Place." And I say, "Oh yeah, I have postcards of 'Bill's Place.' Color and black-and-white. In fact, that's the very picture." Jean is astonished and tells me that "Bill's" *was* just up the hill where the guardrail ends. I begin thinking to myself, not quite ready to salivate, "*was*." Jean continued to tell me that "Bill's" is no longer. Gone. Forever. I start discussing the book project and she gets excited. She tells me about her waitressing days at roadstops, and then Pat strolls in and tells me about her waitressing days. Jean has a flash and decides to call Blanche.

"Who's Blanche?"

"Blanche worked for Bill. She's a bit older—maybe in her early seventies. She'll tell ya about Bill."

Jean calls Blanche, tells her about me and that we are old friends, sends me a quick wink, and I'm on the phone with Blanche. Jean broke the ice for me. I start asking her about Bill and his "place." There is some reticence. Blanche is too old to scream, but old enough for extreme

reverence. I could tell at one time there was a love-hate relationship, and perhaps a skeleton or two in the kitchen cabinet. Blanche says he was well thought of, and I wonder by whom. The tourists? The locals? The cooks and waitresses? Blanche continued, "Bill wanted you to work for nothing. . . ." I was beginning to get the picture. Blanche went on and told me that Bill had died about a year ago, and I could hear in her voice that she didn't want to divulge much more personal information. God bless Bill, eh? She wanted to escape from the conversation, but I wouldn't let her. She wanted me to call Hattie Fix, who waitressed for Bill; Hattie would tell me *more* about Bill and his "place." She closed the conversation with a chuckle telling me about the post office. It was the smallest in the country—two by four feet. I asked Blanche if it *really* was the smallest, and she replied in a long telephone smile, "Well, there's one a few inches smaller."

Arkansas Motel

Was the "Arkansas Motel" painted by one of the Surrealists? By an architectural "renderer"? By a trained camouflage expert? No, just by another printing-plant retouch artist. (Did he paint in the Mighty Mississippi on his own accord, or was this art-directed by the motel owner? We'll never know.) The area surrounding the "Arkansas Motel" needed help—oh, yes indeed—and it still does forty years later.

I was showing the postcard to the recent managers, Lottye and Thomas Allen Burnett, and asked them about this extreme and brutal retouch job. I asked Lottye if she thought this "art" made the motel appear more "romantic." She said, "Oh . . . it probably *was* at one time." She looks outside. "You see the flowers I planted out there? Honey, I worked awful hard to have those few posies."

Thomas picks up the card and takes a good look.

"That's a linen finish!"

"How do you know all that?" I ask.

"I used to be in printing. Those linens, they used to be expensive to print."

"Did you print postcards?"

"No, I printed business letterheads, cards, commercial stuff like that."

"But you know about printing postcards."

"Oh yeah, *they're* commercial."

And we go on and he tells me more about the printing business. He coughs. Thomas tells me about his illness for a year, and how he thought he got sick from being in the printing business. He attributes it all to the powdered spray that is applied to sheets after they come off the press to keep the sheets tight. He's afraid it got into his lungs. As he's telling me this dreadful story, he pulls drag upon drag on a filter cigarette.

Coughing, Thomas said, "We still have old cards; we're keeping them."

I jump. "Where are they?" He reaches down into a drawer and pulls out a chrome finish card. The exact image. We talk about the "linen" art and compare the quality of the paper stock and the color differences with the chrome-coated stock.

After this discussion, I wander around the office and take note that there are four or five signed tile illustrations imbedded in concrete block that's been painted at least twenty-seven times since 1941. They are all of a Mexican theme, and signed by a local Mexican

artist. (Bullfighting was his one passion, of course!) Lottye said the original owner liked Mexico. You bet—the furniture is Mexican in origin, and it's been through many siestas. I can't imagine what the original owner would have done, if he had had the money in those days, to have carried through all the way with the Mexican theme—in Arkansas.

Another roll of the head and eyeballs, and behind the registration desk is a young child's drawing. A self-portrait of the child done for her great-grandmother, Lottye. Written on the drawing in the upper-left-hand corner is "love you I."

Stop Agan

When I first purchased the "Stop Agan" card, I wondered about the name: Agan. I figured that whoever painted the sign forgot to put an "I" between the "A" and the "N." I mean, "Stop Again" is a rather logical name for a commercial enterprise. Why not?

After World War II, L. E. Agan opened a gas station with a World War II surplus training plane, a Cessna "Bobcat," atop the station. He followed with three or four more stations around town—all with aircraft atop the roof. L. E. Agan had a promotional personality and a good advertising sense.

Daughter-in-law Jane was telling me that they used to have another old aircraft sitting on poles off the road on the other side of town. It had a sign that read, "Stop Agan Service." She said the police would get constant calls from people saying a plane had crashed. They had to remove it.

I asked about the rabbit and its significance. She said there were a lot of giant rabbits on the road in West Texas and that they come out at night alot. The rabbit still stands where the old station was, but the place is now a pawn shop. She said the original rabbit was made out of wire and sheepskin, but the newer one is concrete.

I asked L. E. Agan's grandson, Howard Teel, why the rabbit was sitting out in front of the station. "It's a landmark," he replied. And I asked him why use a *rabbit* to attract motorists. He said, "It's just an idea." Then I asked him where the idea came from and Howard replied, "Where all ideas come from—your head."

—STOP AGAN SERVICE—HI-WAY 67 WEST - TEXARKANA, TEXAS

West Highway 67 — STOP AGAN SERVICE — Texarkana, Texas

Moonlight Court

Jane and I are on our way to Manchester, Tennessee, to see how a small, quintessential southern town has changed since two 1943 postcards. Zooming down the road I see at 9 o'clock a stone-faced, double-gabled tavern and I turn to Jane and say, "That's a nice place." I pass it off and she screams, *"That's the Moonlight!"* I do an instant one-eighty and we pull up. It doesn't look like the postcard image, but it *sure* is. (There was a slight facelift that had to jell.)

MOONLIGHT COURT, USA - MANCHESTER, TENN.

I walk in and show Mr. Bartender the card. He says, "What's that?" and I say, *That* is *this* . . . right here where you are standing . . . behind the bar . . . right here." He is perplexed, and we walk over to a table where two men and a woman are seated, all in relaxed positions.

It's about one in the afternoon, but I think this crew are leftovers from the previous evening, or weekend. They're downing beer and looking at the card in fuzzy dismay. A whiskered, disheveled man in his fifties looks at the card attentively and says, "That's unusual. Can I have this?"

I promptly tell him no, and then we get into a discussion of *why* I have the card, and *why* he can't have it. He refuses to listen.

We meet. His name is Ladd Jacobs, and he owns the tavern. His father owned the tourist court.

Ladd keeps saying, "I want this. Can I have it?" I take the card from his puppy-like hand in fear for its future life. I told Ladd I'd make Xeroxes and send some copies.

"I don't care if you make a thousand copies, just give me six. Say, ya'll want a beer; we got plenty of beer . . ."

Ladd takes the card from my hand again, and he says, "I want this, I want to show it to my six kids."

I told him I'd make as many copies as he wanted. Then we went outside so I could catch a few frames in my camera, and everybody is posing, and the woman is calling me "Babe," and the other goof-ball is calling me "Fella," and the bartender is going along for the ride, and Ladd is trying to tell me about the tourist court. He couldn't remember much; he was too wasted. He pointed to three "Pan-Am" gas pump globes imbedded into the stone wall above the gable and said they were sixty years old. He pointed up the road and told us how he used to run booze for fourteen years; he pulled out a paper bag from inside his shirt. In it was a pint of George Dickel Bourbon. (What is this? Prohibition at his own tavern?) He offers us a slug, and natch we refuse, and natch he's offended. We drove off, and I was wondering if the original name for the "Moonlight" was the "Moonshine." It seems pretty proper for a tourist court.

July, 1981

Hoge's

Bonnie and Paul Tilton now own "Hoge's Drive-In." It's a restaurant now—no more drive-in. They've been there since the first of April, 1981. Bonnie looked at the postcards and said, "Wished it still looked that good." She told me that her sister used to work at Hoge's in earlier days and she used to go there a lot when she was a teenager. Donna McHenry, who was waitressing at the time, after viewing the cards said, "Look how funny it looks. Hoge lived here with his two sons. They lived back there where the dining room is. . . . The original 'Hoge's' was out on Dresden Avenue. It's still there. It's called 'Don's Steak Out.'" Donna seemed like she knew a lot. She continued.

"You ought to talk to Pearl. She's my mother-in-law. She started at 'Hoge's' when she was real young. She's about forty-seven now. She owned the place and just left three months ago when Bonnie and Paul bought it from her."

I keep listening to Donna, and now I'm munching on a pretty good hamburger. Hot and juicy.

"Yeah, 'Hoge's' used to be an old roadhouse. I hear there were a lot of wild women here. Then someone got stabbed, and they closed it down. It was dry around here after the Depression. It stayed closed for a long time. Then it was the 'Chatterbox.' Bill Hoge still comes in for a cup of coffee. . . . You ought to call Pearl. I think she's home now. She's fixing to go on vacation; better call her soon."

I call Pearl. She's very receptive, but anxious to get moving on her trip and doesn't have a lot of time to yak. She said "Hoge's" was originally constructed around 1900, and the existing structure goes back to 1905. It was called the "Lincoln March," and there was a lot of gambling and bootlegging and cockfighting. Then, lots of raids.

She continued, "I have lots of memories. A lot of them. I started peeling potatoes when I was twelve-and-a-half. Then I was a coleslaw cutter, then I waited on the counter, and then tables. I bought it from Hoge in 1969. And sold it last April to the Tiltons." Pearl had to leave. She mentions a newspaper article written about her and the restaurant and said she'd forward a copy.

Hoge's Drive-in Restaurant   3 miles west of E. Liverpool, O.   Routes 7 & 30

Hoge's Drive-in Restaurant   3 miles west of E. Liverpool, O.   Routes 7 & 30

This unique Drive-In greets visitors at the Gateway to Pennsylvania's "Peninsula Park", Erie, Pa., where a million visitors each summer frolic on the public beaches or fish in the waters of Lake Erie and Presque Isle Bay.

The Big Fish

John Byrnes, ex-Marine and now a trooper at Peninsular Park, had a few savory words about his memories of the "fish."

"A bunch of us would sneak around the back and buy a bag full of french fries for a dollar. I know, that seemed like a lot of money back then, but the bag full was as large as a grocery bag. That was probably back in the fifties sometime; I can't remember exactly when. . . . That's a great card. I never saw it. . . . Yeah, that's a screen door; they had two screen doors. It was a building; the fish was flat. Painted like a movie set. It was an appetizing place. They had blue pike and yellow pike. Yeah, the fish was deep fried, and they gave you a heaping order all wrapped in paper and served with radishes and scallions and long thick french fries. . . . I'm young, late thirties, and those *were* the good ol' days. Sounds like a cliché, but it's true. One night a bunch of kids were pranking around and stole the tail after closing; that was the beginning of the end. . . .I remember one of the girls I went to grade school with worked there. Her name was Shirley Shell."

Today a red-plastic-roofed-yellow-painted-cinder-block hot-dog bastion stands where the "Big Fish" hung out. Dean Nacopoulis has operated the "Peninsular Gateway Dairy" (3 Hot Dogs $1.39—Greek Sauce) for six years.

The Teapot

Teapots and their kin, coffeepots, adorned our highways and byways in giant form years ago. Pre-Oldenburg-period victual stands still hang around in a bizarre almost prehistoric fashion. The "Teapot" is one of them. Hotdogs, souvenirs, postcards, and cigarettes don't come belching from the little windows anymore. The "Teapot" stands forlorn, doused in a gloomy, peeling, brown-and-white color scheme. But it's still there, and that's important to me. And that's important to the present owners. And it's important for all the roadside freaks who think this type of architecture is hip.

Alice and Cecil Fletcher now own the "Teapot," which

The TEAPOT Carolina Ave. Chester, W. Va.

has been around for about fifty years. Chester, West Virginia, used to be the pottery capital of the country until the early- to mid-fifties when business started to take a tumble. The "Teapot" was a symbol that represented the town's prestige. Cecil was a kiln placer and retired and had nothing to do. They bought it from its previous owner, Mrs. Willfred Devon. "Babe," Mrs. Devon's husband, built it. Alice and Cecil got tired of the red and white and painted it brown and white. Age has scarred its surface, and it needs repair again. The "Teapot" is vacant and ghostlike. The Fletchers told me they want to fix it up and sell souvenirs again. Cecil remarked, "I should paint the damned thing, but there's too many other things to do." His attitude reflects its weariness. I asked Cecil, "Why don't you paint it red and white again, and serve hot-dogs, and sell postcards, like the old days?" He replied emphatically, "I like the color brown!" That was the end of that.

The Fletchers still sell china goods and gift items and doodads you might notice stuck on a secretary's desk or home on the refrigerator door. In the back of the store, a florist was beginning to flourish. I think the Fletchers, and the florist, and the "Teapot" will survive, with proper attention and love. Mrs. Fletcher took one last look at the "Teapot" card (vintage early forties) and asked me if I knew where she could print cards. I gave her the information and wished her well; I guess that early card was inspiration for a new start.

ART LACEY'S BOMBER STATION
The only one in the world---6 mi. so. of Portland, Ore., on 99E

The Bomber

I was looking at some "preemo" postcards of my friends (and postcard-dealers) Newly West and Don Preziosi, going through their "gas station" category. A photocard of a B-17 bomber gas station flashed in front of me. I had spasms.

After calming down, I realized that the experience was similar to a three-ring circus: in one ring was the concept of using the legendary "Flying Fortress" of World War II fame, linked in the second ring was the meshing of the aircraft and the gas station, and in the third ring was a spectacular photocard that was used for advertising and promotional purposes, which is what the entire idea was all about. A triple whammee. I aggressively asked Don if I could someday make a photo copy for my collection, and he gladly obliged.

About nine months later, I am finally making the photo copy (it's for this book) and at the same time am on the phone with Art Lacey, visionary, promoter, tough businessman, and owner of "The Bomber" gas station, restaurant, and motel. I am only sorry I couldn't have made a pilgrimage to the "complex" and met Art in person, because I would be on "cloud-nine" with his sound gas, food, and lodging idea.

I have an affinity for World War II aircraft; in fact, when I was a kid building model planes, the B-17 was one of the first models I tackled, thanks to a wooden "Strombecker" kit, now as rare as a real life B-17, like Art's.

Art Lacey has been answering questions about his "complex," and the B-17, for about thirty-five years. He doesn't tire in his efforts and his love of the business. He was patient, courteous, and truly interested in my concern. We talked about the early days when he started the station with only five pumps. Today he has forty-eight all computerized, and they spew close to five million gallons of gas into auto and truck tanks. I am sure, and of course Art is, too, that's more than any gas station in the country.

I thought Art was a crack pilot during the war, especially on B-17s. "No, I was an engineer. I only flew single engine planes, and considered myself a poor pilot." Art went on and began to tell me the saga of the B-17, flying it from Altus Air Base in Oklahoma to Portland, Oregon. It was in 1947, and B-17s were in storage for a couple of years. They were leftovers subcontracted to Lockheed for manufacture and never saw any service. Art wanted to use the plane as an "advertising stunt," to put up over his gas station. He plunked down $13,750 for the aircraft—the best investment Art ever made, and that was a lot of greens in 1947.

"I rounded up a crew of local farmhands and unpickled the plane to prepare it for flight. We knew nothing about navigation, and I never flew a four-engine ship before, and I had never seen a B-17 except in pictures."

Art is a man full of determination, and even though he was inexperienced behind the controls, he was going to get the old bird back to Portland, single-handed. Regulations required a co-pilot, so Art found a mannequin and put it in the co-pilot's seat, complete with flight cap. He admitted to being frightened and then took off for a test run that ended in a "wheels-up" crash landing.

Art unintentionally destroyed another B-17 in a belly landing; this time the landing gear wouldn't go down. The two planes were "written off" as wind damaged. Art persisted, and on the third go-around he decided

to take two pilot friends with him, which was a smart move; however, his determination forced him to take his parachute and nail it shut in a box. Art was going to take the bird all the way to the ground, hell-or-highwater.

They hit a blinding snowstorm over the Sierra Nevadas, and as his buddies slept he dropped altitude to get below the storm. While doing so he came within inches of hitting a mountain broadside. He literally pulled out of that snag through some expert airmanship, and possibly with the help of greater forces. Because of this weather mess they became lost and buzzed a tiny town to read the roadsigns. After this primal navigation and a few other crazy sweeps, they learned they were one hundred miles off course. They flew treetop level, following railroad tracks, to Klamath Falls, Oregon, where they landed and gassed up for the final trek to Portland. Another storm took them by surprise, and Art took the aircraft to the top of the storm, then pulled down to eight hundred feet, and landed at an airport in Troutdale, Oregon.

This is a brief account of their harrowing flight, but Art went on to tell me that getting the plane across town to Milwaukee, Oregon, was almost tougher than the long cross-country flight. He had trouble with the local authorities—from the Highway Department to the Governor. He never got a permit, but with his genius audacity loaded the plane on four trucks and moved on. He was fined ten dollars for an overwide load. What a joke.

Four years before Art's brilliant idea, he had his wife, his baby daughter, his broken-down car, and $54. Now, Art has a grand life, and he owes it all to his vision, and the B-17. I believe Art is a true American pioneer, and a rare breed of person. He has a value system I admire and respect. He knows what he wants and gets it, no matter what. Art told me he lives by a motto: "You stick and stay and you'll make it pay." Fine words. Art's made it pay all right; he's made a fortune.

Art told me he was going to send a new set of postcards of "The Bomber," and he asked me to come out and visit, assuring me of a place to stay. I can't wait.

ADMIRAL'S LOUNGE

KID BLAIR'S SHOW BOAT

BLUE PLATE 75
Chicken & Lobster Dinners
ALES, WINES & LIQUORS

THE ONLY LAND GOING BOAT IN THE WORLD

SHOW BOAT

MARTY

MARTY'S SHOWBOAT

MARTY'S SHOWBOAT - THREE LAKES, WIS.   Rice Maid Photo

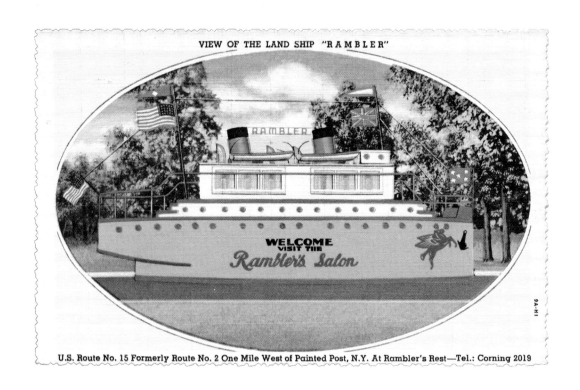

VIEW OF THE LAND SHIP "RAMBLER"

WELCOME
VISIT THE
Rambler's Salon

U.S. Route No. 15 Formerly Route No. 2 One Mile West of Painted Post, N.Y. At Rambler's Rest—Tel.: Corning 2019

Weismantel's Showboat, 808-20 Jamaica Ave., Near Crescent St.
(Telephone Applegate 7-9853) Cypress Hills, N. Y.

WEISMANTEL'S CASINO RESTAURANT

RED SAILS INN
"Sea food Center"
An eating place that
is different

RED SAILS INN

654 HARBOR DRIVE — FISHERMEN'S WHARF — FOOT OF G STREET — SAN DIEGO, CALIFORNIA

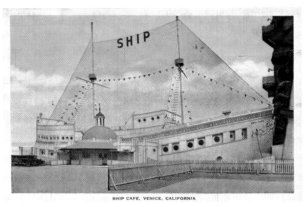

SHIP

SHIP CAFE, VENICE, CALIFORNIA

S. S. GRAND VIEW POINT HOTEL, THE ONLY STEAMBOAT IN MOUNTAINS IN U. S.

GRAND VIEW POINT HOTEL

SEE 3 STATES and 7 COUNTIES

ON U. S. 30, 17 MILES WEST OF BEDFORD, PA.

3A-H777

63 Mile Panorama View from S. S. Grand View Point Hotel on Lincoln

PA.   MD.

GRAND VIEW POINT HOTEL

SEE 3 STATES and 7 COUNTIES

17 Miles West of Bedford, Pa., Looking into 3 States and 7 Counties

GRAND VIEW POINT HOTEL

SEE 3 STATES and 7 COUNTIES   VISITORS WELCOME FREE TELESCOPE

25   GRAND VIEW POINT ON LINCOLN HIGHWAY, 17 MILES WEST OF BEDFORD, PA.   1147-30

GRAND VIEW POINT.
17 M W OF BEDFORD PA
ELEV. 2465 FT.

LOOKOUT POINT GRAND VIEW
ALLEGHENY MOUNTAINS
ELEVATION 2464 FT.

LOOKOUT POINT GRAND VIEW.
17 M. W. OF BEDFORD, PA. U.S. 30.

S. S. GRAND VIEW POINT HOTEL
A Steamer in the Allegheny Mountain.   Seventeen Miles West of Bedford, Pa., U. S. 30.

S.S. Grand View

I've always wanted to visit the "Grand View Point Hotel," the "Grand View Ship Hotel," "The Ship of the Alleghenies Restaurant," the "Ship Hotel," and now, yes, now: "Noah's Ark." Hark, another name for this grandiose roadside, mountainside, hillside spectacle. The new name was coined by the three-year owners May and Jack Loya.

"Noah's is decked out in a wood frame facade, partially complete, but getting there," Jack was telling me at the bar of the famous tourist spot. Jack said they were waiting to furnish the exterior so it will really "look like an ark." As he was taking me around the main dining room and pointing to the original "marine" oil paintings that are like friezes along the walls, he mentioned that he and his wife are desperately trying to save the place. "It's a matter of economics; the tourists don't come around like they used to. The gas crunch has a lot to do with the new road habits, and besides those who do travel take the interstates." The same old story again.

Whatever name it goes by, depending on one's age group, the "Ark" has been jutting out of the mountainside at 2464 feet above sea level for half a century. One card listed the elevation at 2468; Jack told me it was 2998, which sounds impossible. If you look at the sign on the roof of "Minich's Place" it reads: 2906. After visiting Jack, and getting the scoop on the "Ark," I jaunted up the hill to the top, where I hoped there'd be some remnants of "Minich's Place." Somewhere in time everything was erased; there was no trace or evidence of this great gas, food, and lodging image.

Across from "Noah's Ark" -
Grandview Point Service Sta.
July, 1981

Tour-Rest

I was curious about the "Tour-Rest" motel and how it got its name. "Tourist" motel is pretty simple. There are plenty of those. "Tour-Rest" is simple, too. Take your tour and rest. Easy. Obvious. Should it have been named: "Tour-Rest-Mo-Tel"? Or, "To-Rest-Mo-Tel"? I never found out the real facts. The man who originally built the place was in a nursing home. I didn't want to bother him.

The "Tour-Rest" is still around, going strong with the same name. It's been through several owners during the past years. The last owner was moving out the day we arrived. Her husband had died two weeks earlier at the local bar in Waterloo, Indiana. Guess it was time for her to be moving on.

So much for the "Tour-Rest" motel. We headed in to and out of Waterloo. Suddenly while crossing the tracks I had two visual hits at 3 o'clock. Quick—an automatic U-turn. One was the barber shop that was obviously an early, and itsy-bitsy, gas station. The next visual blast was a yellow and black and red neon EAT sign perched high on a dumb brick building. Pure, mint, and old, and a "What's-it-doing-there?" feeling.

We exit the car; Jane goes to the brick building, which has a low-profile junk business going downstairs, and I hightail it to the snipping parlor. Walt Halslip owns the one-chair barbershop and he's scissoring away at a man's hair. (If you can't watch a haircut, have one.) There wasn't much hair, and it didn't look like it needed cutting —just something to do. We start talking about the "Tour-Rest" motel and I pass the card by their eyeballs. They nod. It's acknowledged. Not too much comment. Then soon some gossip about the owners it has been through. It didn't seem as though it had an esteemed reputation. Then we talk about the old gas station that became the liquor and package store that became the laundry that became the barbershop.

Abruptly, in a sudden flash, Jane storms in asking, "Who's Boney?" The man in the chair doesn't look up, eyes fixed straight, not even looking at Jane, and non-chalantly says, "That's me." And Jane says, "They tell me at the junk store that you own that same building and maybe you'd sell the EAT sign. . . . !" I turn around dumbfounded and do a double-drool. Boney says, "Let me finish my haircut and we'll talk about it. It's my birthday today; I'm seventy-five. Maybe I'll go out to dinner,

nothing special. . . ." I look at Jane gleaming and figuring it's my birthday too, because I'm going to fetch that EAT sign and drive home with it.

About an hour later, after some perspiration from inside and from the skies above, I put some greens into Floyd Bonecutter's pocket, wish him a happy birthday, and move on.

June, 1981

TOUR-REST MOTEL

AAA

U. S. HIGHWAY 27 - WATERLOO, INDIANA

TOMORROW'S HOTEL TO-DAY

SHANGRILA MOTEL
ON U. S. 63 AT EDGE OF THAYER, MO. AND MAMMOTH SPRING, ARK.

TRUE REST COUR...

CHAT-N-REST

Rip Van Winkle MOTEL

MOTEL CHAT 'N REST

Sleepy U MOTEL VACANCY

On U. S. Highways 6 & 40. 35 Miles West of Denver ... IDAHO SPRINGS, COLORADO

KAT-O-LOG MOTEL COURT

TIP-TOP MOTEL

U. S. HIGHWAY 54 - EAST SIDE OF EUREKA, KANSAS

Ace Motel   U. S. 30 EAST
CENTRAL CITY, NEBR.

Handy Motel

LM
Lucky Motel

LUCKY MOTEL VACANCY

E. V. Motel
718 HIGHWAY 90 WEST, SAN ANTONIO, TEXAS

Hi Ho Motel
1233 E. 4th St. (U. S. 40)
RENO, NEVADA

Doo Dee Auto Court
In West Part of Scottsbluff, Nebraska, on Highway 26

SPIC-N-SPAN CABINS—FINEST ON THE HIWAY.   U. S. ROUTE 20—4 MILES EAST OF PAINESVILLE, OHIO   B-624

RYDE - NO - MORE CABINS   —   ETNA, MAINE

Ditty Wah Ditty

What's in a name? What's in a motel name? If you had a motel, what would you name it?

"Snoozette-Roomettes." "Catch-Sum-Zees." "Roll-N-Hay Courts."

What about "Ditty Wah Ditty? Wouldn't that arouse your curiosity chords? It did mine. We set out on a sabbatical to Memphis, Tennessee, to check-it-out—but not to check-in.

Route 51S (in Memphis) is now named Elvis Presley Boulevard. I wasn't too surprised entering the strip—fast food heaven, used-car heaven, all the usual strip stuff. There's a ghastly sight of funny-looking people gathered around a gate. The gate has musical notes embroidered on it. This is Graceland? It's Graceland. Fooled like everyone who "doesn't know," I thought Graceland was in the boonies, and frankly I didn't care where it was. It *was* the boonies. Route 51S was a two-laner, in the woods, which accounts for the reason why the "Ditty Wah Ditty" was in the area. Motels of this type were always on the outskirts of cities, far "off-the-beaten-track."

Where did "Ditty Wah Ditty" get its name? I am getting obsessed. Across from Graceland it looks like an RV convention. Upon closer look it's a shopping center. No, it's not a shopping center, it's "Graceland Center." It *was* a shopping center; now it's a rip-off center with about a dozen shops selling Elvis junk. Vultures in aid of greed. I look for people who may give a clue to the "Ditty Wah Ditty." I locate Lewis Harris, a security guard for Graceland Center. He's friendly as the dickens; and starts talking about the "Ditty Wah Ditty" motel. Lewis says, "We have a lot of peoples 'round-cher.' I ain't never seen that before. I been here since I was nine. Tell you what to do; go across the street and talk to Harold Loyd, the guard at the gate. He'll know, he's been there for twenty years. He's Elvis's cousin. He'll know. Good luck. Wait, lemme give you my address; you gotta let me know."

Jane and I traipse across the street. It's 95 degrees and we're mugged out, but determined. We have to wiggle our way through the K-Mart-styled cellulite crowd. No Izods here, only transfer T-shirts. I am patient and wait for Harold to finish one of the hundreds of Elvis stories he constantly tells the gatecomers. (He's already written a book about the gate people.) I introduce myself, show him the card, and we get down to "Ditty Wah Ditty" biz.

Harold didn't know the answer, but he said the motel is still around under a different name. (Was that the real "Heartbreak Hotel"?) He directed us north a few miles—"keep looking on your right, it's there."

Vrooom, up the road, eyes right. Time has deposited its seeds, the decay is held up by a hot-July-Saturday-evening-life of drive-ins, a couple of beer palaces, and motels. We pass the "Elvis Presley Boulevard Inn Home of Good Foods and Lodging." Who are they kidding? On up the road, nothing happens. Trees and shrubs grow up like people when their faces and bodies change. Was the motel masked by all this foliage? One decrepit motel looks familiar. It's a scratch. Onward, slowly. There's a foothill that resembles the driveway in the card. There are a couple of young ladies prancing around. Cars are stopping and talking to them. I get suspicious, but I've got to ask questions. Highway hookers in action; they goofed when I showed them the card. One starts a mini-dance, singing "Ditty Wah Ditty, Ditty, Ditty." They direct me to the motel. We drive up, and yes: it's the "Ditty Wah Ditty"! Now called the "Iris."

The person that owns the motel is "away." I talk to next-in-charge. She's a large woman—an ex-Big Mama wearing many pink hair curlers, and smoking a long, pencil-like cigar. She talks in a microphone through a window. Her voice is muffled. I pass the card through the window, and she gets interested in "Ditty Wah Ditty." She gets busy with a customer; I move over one step for this man.

"What kinda car you in?"

"Uh . . . I'm on a motorcycle. She's in a car."

"OK, sign here."

I'm looking around during this break. A brightly lettered sign reads: "I HR.—$8.00," "2 HR.—$9.00," and goes on hour-by-hour up to twelve hours (wheeeew!) for $34.00. I look up, and another sign reads: "Radio—25¢." There were three-step instructions on how to use the radio.

The transaction has been conducted, and I am back to my biz. Big Mama hands me a business card for the "Iris Motel." Written on the card is the name of the manager. She said to call him, that he may have the answer for me. I called and I wrote, and nothing.

Then, magically, a communique arrived from Jane and Michael Stern. It was a Xeroxed page from *A Bowl of Red* by Frank X. Tolbert (Doubleday, 1972). Hidden in the recesses of his book is the following:

In folklore, Didy Waw Didy (sometimes spelled Ditty Wah Ditty) was the last stop on a mythical railroad bound for hell. And there's an old song made famous by Phil Harris, with the refrain:

It ain't a town and it ain't a city—
Just a little place called Didy Waw Didy:

Was I getting a close answer? I couldn't exactly tell. Then I put on Ry Cooder's album, "Paradise and Lunch." On the last band of side two is a long and extremely melodic number sung by Cooder and accompanied by the master himself, Earl "Fatha" Hines. Listen to it. Listen to "Ditty Wa Ditty."

Constance Bernard, Owner

DITTY WAH DITTY
TOURIST COURT
MEMPHIS, TENNESSEE

U. S. Highway 51, South

Mammy's Cupboard

For forty-nine years, every March in Natchez, Mississippi, there has been a tour of historic homes. It is called "The Pilgrimage." Local resident Mrs. H. J. Gaude wanted to serve sandwiches and drinks to the pilgrims, but she wanted to do it in true, traditional antebellum style. Mrs. Gaude went to her husband Henry, who had a Shell gas station, and asked him for an idea.

Henry J. Gaude drew his wife a little picture of a "mammy," and that was the birth of "Mammy's Cupboard." She is still young—forty-two years old. And twenty-eight feet tall. And through the years she has become the grande dame of Natchez society. Her "cupboard" is in her crinoline and covers a twenty-foot area. It was the perfect combination for the pilgrims: Mrs. Gaude served her southern victuals and Mr. Gaude served his gasoline and oil. Mildred Vedreene now keeps the cupboard stocked and serves short orders. She's the wife of Gaude's nephew.

"Mammy" is *not* just another "interesting" commercial building. Gaude is an artist of immense resources. He built "Mammy" out of love, a deep sense of American history, and with his own hands. He took materials from an old cotton warehouse—cypress beams travel the length of the dome. He crafted the twelve-foot torso from tin. And he gives "Mammy" a facelift of paint every two years. I feel Gaude is an artist who comes from true folk-art tradition and that he, too, should not be forgotten.

MAMMY'S CUPBOARD, NATCHEZ, MISSISSIPPI

This beautiful GULF SERVICE STATION in Bedford, Pa. on Lincoln Highway, U.S. 30, 100 miles east of Pittsburgh

Dunkle Gulf

I cruised into Bedford, Pennsylvania, on a sleepy Sunday in a sleepy town. I pass through looking for a special Gulf station but find a special taxi station that resembles a miniature log cabin. I figure the Gulf station isn't around, because if it is it's too good to be true. And, besides, I'm hungry; I need food-fuel, and all that was available was a Burger King that looked as if it was erected the night before. I jaunt across town and give a try on their new chicken sandwich. (McDonald's already has this burger replacement and high-profit item, so I try the competition.) Oh, it was steaming hot-hot-hot, masking any deep-fried-herb-infested flavor making an attempt to seep out on my palate. I still ended up with cardboard breath, the curse of fast-food emporiums.

June, 1981

I decided to give Bedford another try—one more visual hit on those sleepy streets. Drive, drive, look right, look left, drive, drive, look right, look left, ahhhhhh, there it is, the Gulf station. I couldn't believe it! A trip into my own, my *very* own fantasy world. This is really IT for me, the postcard experience, the desire to "go back into a postcard" on a three-dimensional level—the highest, most elegant form. A shocking experience. Up goes the heartbeat.

Gas stations of this variety (and there are plenty of them, but maybe not many documented on postcards) are normally reserved for personal archives. They end up in articles about early gas stations, art-deco architecture, and the "look-what-a-cool-photographer-I-am" books. I was curious about this station because I feared it had been replaced by a slick, new Gulf station, and I wanted to experience the contrast. Or perhaps a Pizza Hut. (I was still hungry) Or a twenty-four hour laundromat. (For Bedford's insomniacs.) I wanted to face my fear on this corner in Bedford, Pennsylvania. I was given a surprise, and my fantasy was fulfilled.

The station was closed, and I asked around town about the owner. Several days later I telephoned Jack Dunkle. At first he didn't have much to say; that is, he didn't want to talk—he thought I was a salesman. We soon got into conversation and he became enthusiastic and friendly, and quickly we were onto the same wave length. We talked like old buddies. Jack is thirty-four and had assumed management of the gas station in 1975. His dad had been in the business for fifty-two years. Jack said his dad had hundreds of stories, but he died in 1979.

I asked Jack for one.

"A lot of people come passing through and stop their cars, get out, and take pictures. One day a couple of years ago—you know, this is kind of a hick town—a good-looking lady got out of a car, walked over close to the building, did a frame with her hands, and said real loudly: 'art deco!' and walked back to her car and drove off."

Like myself, Jack is an old-car nut, and we talked about our mutual passion for collecting old cars, and gas station memorabilia. While on the subject, I had a post-card of "The Coffee Pot" in Bedford, Pennsylvania, in front of me. I asked Jack about the place and the gas station that was adjacent to this marvel of a roadside eatery. I assumed it had disappeared into the winds of nostalgia.

With great support in his voice, Jack said:
"You missed that!!!! It's only a stone's throw from here."

I had an empty feeling in my stomach; a postcard heartache; a sudden urge to drive back to Bedford.

"Oh yeah, it's still here. I can't believe *you* missed it. It's still called 'The Coffee Pot,' but it's not open anymore. And the garage isn't in operation."

Jack is feeling my sorrow.

"I'll go down and take a picture of it for you. What's your address?"

Jack was pretty excited that I had an original postcard of his Gulf station. I made a color print of it and we exchanged pictures.

A couple of months roll by and I get a long, friendly letter from stranger Kevin Kutz. On the letter paper is a beautifully drawn self-portrait. (What an introduction.) Kevin is friends with Jack Dunkle and lives close to the station, and that's how he got to me. Kevin is another roadside brother—in fact, at the time he was painting a large canvas of the Gulf station. Everyday he would set up his easel across the street and paint madly, and meticulously. Kevin would pass on many stories from passers-by. ("Whadya wanna paint an old gas station for . . ?" and stuff like that.)

We became fast telephone/mail friends, and Kevin understood my frustration about missing the "Coffee Pot." Within a couple of weeks I received a package in the mail from him, and before opening it I could tell it was loaded with a surprise. In it were several pictures of the current structure.

Kevin's pic – Aug., 1981

THE COFFEE POT
BERT KOONTZ PROP., WEST END FILLING STA., BEDFORD PA.

Now Serving "Genuine" Outdoor Pit Barbecue

GREEN DERBY
BAR-B-Q
CHICKEN
& RIBS
Mexican
Dishes
STEAKS
OPEN
6 A.M.

Green Derby Restaurant
HIGHWAY 80 WEST ON FOUR LANE DRIVE
AT DRAKE MOTEL
JACKSON, MISSISSIPPI

DERBY
CAFE
RESTAURANT

HIGHLY RECOMMENDED BY
DUNCAN HINES
AND BY THE AMERICAN
AUTOMOBILE ASSOCIATION.

CHAMBERLAIN
SOUTH DAKOTA

South Dakota's Finest
DERBY'S CAFE

Brown Derby

Gene Barrett, along with his friend Betty White, is an antique dealer from Owensville, Indiana—about 35 miles north of Evansville, Indiana. I showed him the card of the "Brown Derby Restaurant." His etched and tanned face lit up. "Oh . . . I used to go there a lot. It was a honky-tonk. You'd have to pay a dollar for a Coke. They were expensive because all the big-name bands played there, and they'd have to be paid. It was a no man's land; it burned down in the late forties. There was this other place down the road a bit in Kentucky. It was a gambling place . . . [at this point, I flash the card of the Club Trocadero, and Gene gleams more twinkles in his warm eyes]. Oh, yes, it was high class. They had all kinds of gambling there—all kinds of different rooms. I knew a guy there who'd bet you it would be raining on a nice sunny day if you gave him odds. I saw this guy make ten thousand dollars one evening, and then lose it a few minutes later."

There are many stories on Gene's face. I asked him more about the Club Trocadero, including whether he ever saw the old movie called *The Trocadero*. He hadn't. But, he told me the place still stands in Henderson, Kentucky. The state owns the property. A group of antique dealers wanted to open a mall in the old building, but the state turned them down, and it stands vacant today.

Gene continued to tell me how he used to haul limestone 150 miles to Indianapolis, and in those days it took eight hours and the trucks would only get six to seven miles per gallon. He stopped at many gas stations and ate in diners on the way. I began to see more stories on his face. They were itching to be released. I could tell that Gene doesn't talk about those earlier and more tender years on the road. Gene had a customer, and I had to leave him. I felt full, and empty.

CLUB TROCADERO   Henderson, Ky.

BROWN DERBY GRILL — DELICIOUSLY PREPARED FOOD. GOOD COFFEE

30 COTTAGES — PRIVATE BATHS. STEAM HEAT. INNER-SPRING MATTRESSES

Most everybody stops at the MARYANN, ANGOLA, INDIANA

Maryann

After snapping a few shots of the "Dinky Diner" in Angola, Indiana, a small (and dinky) town in northeast Indiana, I notice a man parked in a black Chevy pickup. It has one of those camper tops sitting on the pickup part. I walk over and show him a Xerox of "Maryann's." (I had misplaced the original card.)

"Maryann Hicks. We went to school together."

I introduce myself and tell him of my quest, and Warren Andrews invites me into the truck for some more chat. He's immediately friendly.

"She married a guy from Canada, and I guess she's up there now. Lost track of her. Supposed to be a reunion in August. Angola High, 1941. I hope to see her there, John. There's a coin shop uptown, across from the Post Office, and that's where 'Maryann's' used to be. It was just a little hamburger joint—eaten many a root beer float there."

Warren was parked next to the "Dinky Diner" waiting for a friend. They were going out to have a spaghetti dinner. We talked some more, and he told me about his twenty years driving a semi and the different trucking companies he had worked for. And then we got into the past a bit and back to World War II. Warren was a Tech Sgt. in the 4th Army, 79th Division, when his platoon got wiped out at the Rhine River. He was the only soldier left, with four purple hearts to show for it. And 70 percent disability to show for that.

Warren is an appreciative man. Warm, gentle, and receptive. If we had stuck around, we would still be talking around a spaghetti dinner, and swapping more stories. I am very sure of that.

I like the look of the "Corner Cafe" and had an insatiable curiosity regarding its remains. The "corner" idea intrigued me because my fantasy was that the cafe actually sat in the intersection of Tennessee, Kentucky, and Virginia. Cumberland Gap, Tennessee, is a miniscule town, and as I drove in the cafe slipped by my intense peripheral vision. I felt a sense of loss and rambled into a restaurant and presented the postcard to a few of the hired hands. They were baffled by the picture of the "cafe." They were young and only knew the "cafe" as the post office. Their eyes popped in bewilderment. The ever-famous "seeing-is-believing" concept rang true in their psyches. They directed me around the corner, two tiny blocks away, and also informed me that the actual "corner," or point, where the three states join was about a mile away. I was disappointed at hearing that detail—my fantasy destroyed.

The visual experience was one of those remarkable time-warp moments, moments that enrich life and make one feel their true sense of purpose. Nothing, I mean nothing, had changed. The cafe had been transposed into a post office, sure; the signs came down; that was natural. While taking pictures, I noticed an older couple across the street in a late model Cadillac sedan. They appeared to be tourists taking a break, a driver change. But then I saw them fiddle around with grocery bags. I disregarded them, but was curious about their presence in this amazingly tiny town. I was so energized by the post office and the time-warp quality that I forgave them for the distraction. Then a couple of guys in a new Corvette come strolling by and greet me and the couple in the Cadillac. I figure it as small-town friendliness on a lazy Summer Solstice Sunday evening. More forgiveness.

I continue to snap a few more pics and wander up the street to check out an early drugstore sign. While I was doing so, the same Cadillac approaches me and sharply swings into a driveway across the street. It's the same couple. Card and camera in hand, I hastily approach a well-dressed man getting out of the car. Promptly, and abruptly, I show the postcard to this well-dressed gentleman. He tells me he owns the building and asks if he could first take his groceries into the house. I oblige and get a rush, and then ask him if we can spend some time together. He invites me to the front porch—the kind that's made for perfect lazy summer evenings with perfect lazy summer chairs to match.

J. D. Estep came to Cumberland Gap, Tennessee, in 1906 and built a grocery store in 1919. Business prospered,

Corner Cafe

June, 1981

Corner Cafe - At The Foot Of The Pinnacle - Cumberland Gap Tenn. Ky. Va.

R-274

and in 1926 he built a drugstore across the street. A few years later the Depression was in full force and the drugstore business took a tumble. J. D. said, "I lacked capital . . . we sweated blood every day back then. . . ." Since his drugstore already had a counter, he added some tables and chairs and a kitchen and soon it became the "Corner Cafe." Business was good, Route 23E was a main drag, and the town was larger in those days. J. D. went on to tell me it was a trading center for poultry. He went on, "There were about 750 people in town then; today there's only 200 or so."

J. D. is a warm, soft man who was approaching his eightieth birthday. He looked twenty years younger. We were studying the card together in silence. I could tell he was reflecting. I turned to J. D. and said, "Was the cafe sign blue and white?" He replied, "Yes, how did you know?" I said, "That's how I would have wanted it." I asked J. D. who the man was standing in the doorway. He looked at him, thinking back forty years, and said, "That's Clyde Winter standing there in the doorway . . . he ran the cafe. The cafe went out of business around 1964 . . . there wasn't enough people around and most of the tourist trade stayed on the new Route 23E. . . . It's been a post office for fifteen years now; the lease is up soon and they'll renew it for another fifteen."

I didn't want to leave J. D. Estep, but I could tell it was time to go. I got up from the lazy porch chair, smelled the shrubs and felt a breeze, and heartily shook hands goodbye.

The Real McCoy's

Martha McCoy was a school teacher before she decided to join her husband Donald in the gas station–restaurant business. (That's Martha on the furthest left.) That was in 1945. They had to close down in 1972; the tourists weren't coming around anymore, they were going the interstate routes.

Martha said it was a beautiful tourist stop. Her husband was a natural "advertising man." He would post signs on the road welcoming people to Black River Falls, Wisconsin. All the signs showed a sense of humor, and the people loved them. Donald's sense of public relations,

caring, and wit was followed through on the reverse side of the card. It reads: "Here's the 6 Real McCoys that are gonna try like the dickens to make you glad you stopped in Black River Falls, Wisconsin."

Martha and I talked on the phone for a while. It was like a visit to the restaurant after the lunchtime rush, sitting around a table chatting over a cup of coffee—warm and friendly like the postcard. She told me the name "The Real McCoy's" was patented. I said that was a very smart idea, and she replied:

"My husband knew all kinds of slogans; everybody loved to come here."

I told Martha how much I enjoyed the postcard and how good it made me feel. I asked about her kids.

"My two sons are in Florida, one is in the hardware business, and the other one is in the furniture business; one daughter is in Sparta, Wisconsin, and the other is in the restaurant business in Black River Falls. My husband has died."

I asked, "What happened to the original building?"

"There were two restaurants since we were there. They deteriorated and never did anything. I don't know what's there now. Maybe nothing."

Donald McCoy knew something when he patented "The Real McCoy's," he knew there were plenty of McCoys to go around, just like the old tale about all the boxers named "McCoy." There's only one *real* McCoy.

OKeDoak

The "OKeDoak" is the only remaining early piece of "bygone" architecture on the Dixie Highway, now strip-city, going south from Chattanooga into the Georgia border. I passed the "OKeDoak" and recognized it immediately. I could even tell it needed some petting. I snapped a few pics and was eagerly getting ready to scoot off, but I noticed a figure in a room changing a bed. I was relieved, because I felt anxious to talk to someone and inquire how the "OKeDoak" made it through the years.

I meet Kenneth Lockhart, a mild-mannered and attractive man in his very early thirties. I showed Ken the card, and his immediate response was, "Someone painted and drew on that. . . !" Then I explained to him the linen printing process and the forced color and exaggeration. He seemed a bit relieved, but was still visibly shaken.

Ken began to tell me more about the history of the motel—now turned apartments, by the week and month, and re-named, "The Rock Apts." It was built around 1938, and W.H. Doak owned it during the war. He got ill and mortgaged it to another family, and then it went through a few more owners. Ken's grandfather, William M. Johnson, bought the motel at auction in 1955. Ken has had it since 1973.

Ken got interested in the postcard and the feelings that came from seeing it. I could tell he was moved. He went over to his grandfather's house, which was next door, and came out with a large black and white photograph of the motel with an Esso station and restaurant to the left and his grandfather's home to the right. It was taken around 1949–50 because I noticed his grandfather's 1949 Lincoln "Cosmopolitan" parked to the side. The photo had seen many hands and memories. It was reproduced on a postcard his grandfather used to send to guests and to give away. Ken had the postcard—a black-and-white offset variety—in his other hand, and we were comparing the postcards and the photograph.

Ken is also a devotee of roadside culture, and I observed he doesn't get to talk to many people about the motel and its history. He started in on all the roadhouses that used to exist on the highway, and all the fights and drunken battles. He got into the land that was around the motel and back of the motel. And when I pointed to the McDonald's across the street, Ken said that was where the "Pines Motel and Cabins" used to be. Ken became more than enthusiastic.

We switched back in time; I could tell *that* reality was more appealing to Ken. He knew it was for me. Ken went on to describe tiny fragments about the Esso gas station–restaurant that was attached to the motel—from the grease pit to the details of the restaurant, which became a fruit stand, which became a hot-dog stand. Then the Esso people came by one day and took down the large "Esso" sign, and pulled up the gas pumps. And more details of where the manager's quarters were—now a trophy shop. We re-visited the pool's location, and where the shrubs used to be planted, and the exact location where the lawn furniture stood, and the trees—the trees that were whitewashed.

OKeDOAK TOURIST COURT

7 Miles South of Chattanooga, Tenn. On U.S. 41 & 76

We went back to my linen postcard: Ken became fascinated with it. We were trying to decide where the "pinkish-tone" on the stone came from. Was it just an exercise in "creative-license"? Did Doak himself want his motel to look less bland and for the application of the "reddish-color" to give it some pizzaz? We took a second look at the stonework, and under closer scrutiny there was a "rose" cast to some of the stone. The color was subtle, but it *was* there. Mr. Doak knew that, and he took advantage of postcard exaggeration. I'm sure he asked the printers to add the extra color. Doak was OK.

TOTO'S

NORTHAMPTON · HOLYOKE HIGHWAY

CLOSE COVER BEFORE STRIKING

ZEPPELIN TOURIST CAMP.

EATS

US-30 ON 30 EATS

EATS

POST CARD

TOTO'S ZEPPELIN, New England's Most Unique Restaurant, in the Historic Connecticut River Valley, on Route 5 between Northampton and Holyoke, Mass.
Delicious Food—Choice Liquors—Popular Prices
Dancing and Entertainment

Why not have Sunday Dinner with us? Toto

P.S. Entertainment in Cocktail Lounge every evening

COCKTAIL LOUNGE, TOTO'S ZEPPELIN

83

GREYHOUND UNION BUS TERMINAL, FORT WAYNE, INDIANA

June, 1981

Ft. Wayne Greyhound

Jane and I are visiting her ninety-two-year-old grand-father, E. Yost Braddock, in Columbia City, Indiana. E. Yost boasts of designing a 1913 Indianapolis race car and of working on the engine with auto legend Fred Duesenberg. Yost is quite a man—an inspiration to anyone who complains he is tired, or has a few pains, or can't find anything to do in his retirement. He's a bundle of energy and kicks away every day at the drawing board or in his machine shop with a revolutionary new engine he invented. Yost has a lot to tell, and after I listen to tale after tale I excuse myself and am off to nearby Ft. Wayne, Indiana; I had to check a couple of diners.

Ft. Wayne is home of the famous "Wayne" and "Tokheim" gas pumps that have served every automobile and truck and bus in America. Ft. Wayne is bustling in the late afternoon rush hour, and I can't locate the diners. I'm squaring one-way streets and bucking foreign traffic. Whoooa . . . my third eye notices a blue mass of art-moderne wonderment. Quickly it comes into focus. There it is, the "old" Greyhound station, magically lifted from the postcard image I had tucked away. It was akin to watching a magician doing a disappear-reappear trick. Very shocking.

The station was boarded-up, in need of a shower, shave, and shine. Not quite ready for the "row," but close. It had some life in it, and thanks to its owner, local attorney Joe Christoff, it will have new life again. There are people like Joe who have the foresight, vision, and motivation to save the life of a building like the Greyhound station. Joe isn't a member of any "all-talk-no-action-historic-landmark-preservation" group. Joe *cares*, and he's doing his darndest to give new life back to the station, to let the citizens of Ft. Wayne appreciate and enjoy it as much as he does.

Greyhound hats-off to Joe Christoff.

AUGUST

BUS
TIME TABLES

PACIFIC
GREYHOUND
LINES

COAST TO COAST
BORDER TO BORDER

GREYHOUND *Lines*

DESTROY ALL PREVIOUS ISSUES

SOUTHEASTERN GREYHOUND LINES

PAUSING TO WATCH CLOUD EFFECTS

GREYHOUND
NEW YORK-LOS ANGELES

BESIDE LAKE ALONG ROUTE OF EASTERN GREYHOUND LINES

go GREYHOUND

"This Amazing America"
BEST

RESERVATIONS MAY BE
MADE THROUGH
Postal Telegraph
SEE

FOR
BUSINESS
FOR
PLEASURE
FOR
LESS

go GREYHOUND

U.S. Cafe

When visiting Dalton, Georgia, in search of the "U.S. Cafe," I made the horrendous mistake of arriving on a Sunday. Sunday in a small Southern town is like entering the set of a fifties sci-fi thriller after the population has been evacuated to the mountains—in fear of the fire-breathing monster on its way to destroy the town. The only sign of life was the marquee of the "Wink" theater—it was asking passersby to watch H.B.O.

I talked with Sarye Nochumson, a long-time resident of Dalton, now residing in Atlanta. Sarye has deep affection for the "U.S. Cafe," and Dalton, Georgia, her home for about thirty years. ("They were marvelous people to me . . .") Sarye and her husband Ira moved to Dalton in the very early forties, before the war. Ira, who opened a carpet mill (Dalton is the carpet center of the country.), was a very charitable figure around the city, providing much good for the welfare of its citizens. Sarye said it was a "two by nothing town." But, she didn't mean that in a negative fashion. Sarye, a mid-seventyish, dear, and loving woman, went on to express more affection for Dalton and the "U.S. Cafe."

"Oh, my goodness, we ate there all the time. The buyers would come in from all over the country, and my husband would take them there for breakfast and lunch. Then for dinner they'd come to my home; it was the *best* restaurant. . . ."

I described the interior view on the card to Sarye, and before I could finish she was all excited and said, "Ohhhh, *sure* I remember that card. Very well, indeed. When we would pay the cashier, after our meals, Ira would always take several and put them in his pocket. And I would say to Ira, 'Why do you always take so many cards? What do you do with them?' and Ira told me: after the buyers returned home, he would send them the postcards telling the buyers to come back and visit and he would take them back to the 'U.S. Cafe.' I thought that was so nice of him. He was such a nice man, my Ira."

I asked Sarye if she thought "U.S." in the "U.S. Cafe" stood for United States, as in "U.S. 41," which was the highway that ran through Dalton at the time, or "US," like a mom and pop much in love owned the cafe.

"Oh, my dear, I just don't know. I wish I could help."

So, I dialed the "U.S. Cafe" and spoke to James White, the owner for the past fifteen years. He relieved my bewilderment. James said Ulys and Stone were the names of the original owners when the cafe began operation in 1924.

I thought Ulys an unusual name and asked James how it was spelled. "I don't rightly know, I think it's U-L-Y-E-S. Wait, maybe it's U-L-E-S." And I asked, "What about U-L-I-S?" "Nah, it ain't like that." I figured it had to be U-L-Y-S, short for Ulysses, because this is an odyssey and that's an appropriate name, and an appropriate abbreviation.

U.S. CAFE — DALTON, GA.

NATIONALLY KNOWN

I didn't want to dissect too far; then my fun would be shattered. James went on to tell me some self-history (He used to be in the meat business and is an expert in his field.) and cafe history, mostly about the changes that it has undergone—like the expansion and remodeling that occurred in 1955 when the "U.S." broke through next door to the "City Cafe." (It hasn't changed since, except for new wallpaper.) And we talked at length about the past three owners: Marion Hudgins, Cline Griggs, and Ed King, from whom he bought it. King is now a prominent poultry businessman in Georgia.

Then the climax, as we said our good-byes. In his stereotyped Southern drawl, Jack told me, "Ya knooow, I haave thaat ool caaard you were talking about, iiiits aat home in a draaawer."

That made me very happy.

Most Beautiful
DINER
in Chicago

EAT

the Burlington

BURLINGTON DINER. 4183

RESTAURANT
CIGARETTES

GOOD
FOOD

QUICK
SERVICE

Dutch Diner

"I never saw that before," said Carolyn Wagner when shown the postcard of the "Dutch Diner."

"Skip James used to own it. He lived in a trailer behind the diner. When I was dating my husband we'd go there. I was a waitress at the Shartlesville Hotel, and you know you don't eat the food you serve, so he'd pick me up after work and off we went—it was just across the street."

Carolyn ponders and reflects:

"Yeah, a dear memory. It was sort of a hangout. A very welcome place. We all pulled pranks and joked around a lot. The way you used to when you were younger. You know?" I nodded, "Yeah, I do know, very well. Just exactly where was the diner, Carolyn?"

"Soon as you get to town, go to the end of the first block, and on the corner there's a vacant lot, and next to the lot there's an alley. You can't miss it. That's where the diner used to be."

I drove down and passed the vacant lot. All grassed up and well manicured. I didn't want to look too hard. I glanced. It was like forcing yourself to view a loved one's grave. Why remember someone you loved dearly, someone that was important to you, by peering down at a piece of stone sticking up out of the grass?

I didn't tell Carolyn the significance of the "Dutch Diner." And how the "Dutch Diner" image played a pivotal part in projecting me into a new career that changed my life completely. You see, the "Dutch Diner" was *the* first image I painted when I decided to leave advertising and paint full time—to paint postcard images of gas, food, and lodging. The "Dutch Diner" means a lot to me.

Dutch Diner, 1972
Acrylic on Canvas, 42 × 66", collection Daniel Fillipacci, Paris.

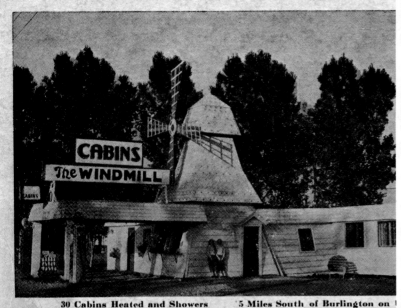

CABINS
The WINDMILL

30 Cabins Heated and Showers   **5 Miles South of Burlington on**
Telephone 2-4296   **C. E. HICKS,**

DUTCH KITCHEN

SILVER CREEK, N.Y.

VAN DE KAMP'S HOLLAND DUTCH BAKERS, LOS ANGELES, CALIF.

TYPICAL WINDMILL BAKERY STORE

WHERE YOU MEET
TO
EAT-
DUTCHLAND
REG. U.S PAT. OFF.

Let's Go to Dutchland

DUTCH MILL
Always a Friendly Welcome
EAST OF MADISON, WISCONSIN

125 MILES EAST OF NIAGARA FALLS, N. Y. ROUTES 5 AND 20

53-30

DUTCH MILL VILLAGE   GLASGOW, KENTUCKY

SHOO-FLY PIES DUTCH HAVEN SHOO-FLY PIES

ACH COME ON IN!

AMISH STUFF

WIGWAM VILLAGE No. 2

1 MILE NORTH OF CAVE CITY ON 31-W

8A-H3035

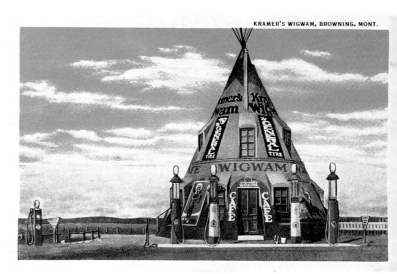

KRAMER'S WIGWAM, BROWNING, MONT.

GERONIMO'S CASTLE — GREYHOUND BUS DEPOT — BOWIE, ARI

LUNCH ROOM, WIGWAM VILLAGE, No. 2

1 MILE NORTH OF CAVE CITY, KY. ON U. S. 31-W

8A-H3036

92

See Kentucky from the Tower Free   Kodachrome by Jack Taylor

Little Dutch Mill, Junction U. S. 31-E at 70.

No. 1 .. HORSE CAVE, KY.
No. 2 ... CAVE CITY, KY.
No. 3 .. NEW ORLEANS, LA.
No. 4 ... ORLANDO, FLA.
No. 5 . BIRMINGHAM, ALA.
No. 6 .. HOLBROOK, ARIZ.
No. 7 . SAN BERNARDINO, CALIF.

THE OHIO MATCH CO., WADSWORTH, OHIO

June, 1981

Wigwam Nº 1

Wigwam No. 1 was torn down in the spring of 1981. I missed the event by a few months. Across the highway is the Wigwam Gulf Station. Glenn Bastin has been there for twenty-five years. One of his coworkers, Bob, looked at the card and said he didn't remember the rail fences. He's been at the Wigwam Gulf for about the same amount of time. Then Kenneth, another coworker, looked at the card and said, "I never seen one of them before." He was in shock viewing this vintage card of the "Wigwam Village."

Glenn went on to tell me that it was built around 1931–32. "It had solid oak furniture and fancy Indian rugs and curtains and bedspreads. . . . Frank Redford, who built and owned all the Wigwam motels around the country (there were around seven if I can remember right . . .); well, he brought in a real Cherokee Indian one day. You shoulda seen that guy; he was parading around with all his feathers. Cocksure, ya know. He was a young man, maybe in his early thirties."

I then showed Glenn and the rest of the grease gang a card of the "Little Dutch Mill," which was located several miles down the road. He told me the Dutch Mill idea was just a gimmick, and the structure was still around but hadn't done any business for about twelve to fifteen years. I drove down and, yes, it looked the same. There were no pumps, no railing, and no windmill. There was a "recreational vehicle" parked mysteriously in front. It didn't make me feel comfortable; and, besides, I wanted to take some pictures of the place and the truck was in the way of my visual. I was talking to A.W. Ross, who is a mechanic for farm equipment. He was in the adjacent building and was rather quiet about the place. He was friendly, but not in a talky mood. He didn't care too much for the chap in the RV. This guy was living in the old station. I wanted to talk to him and get some more scoop on the Dutch Mill. As I thanked A.W. for being nice, but not helpful, I started over to this strange character. I got a few steps, and before I knew it he was off and running in his RV. So we headed off to Wigwam No. 2; which was close by and still going strong.

Ho-Jo

FEDERAL MATCH CORP., NEW YORK

HOWARD JOHNSON'S
FAMOUS
ICE CREAM

RESTAURANTS &
CREAM SHOPS

HOWARD JOHNSON'S

CLOSE COVER BEFORE STRIKING

HOWARD JOHNSON'S

CLOSE COVER BEFORE STRIKING MATCH

New Jersey TURNPIKE

HOWARD JOHNSON'S
· CAMBRIDGE, MASS. ·

JOIN US AT

MENU

★ HOWARD JOHNSON'S ★
delicious food

Howard Johnson's, North Adams, Massachusetts, 1978
Oil on canvas, 30x48", collection Technimetrics Inc., New York, New York.

I had always been hot to paint a Howard Johnson's in a country setting, but couldn't find the right one in the right place. Three years ago I spent some summer time in the Berkshire Mountains in Williamstown, Massachusetts. One day I passed an early Ho-Jo and said to myself, "I will know you better someday. I'll be back." A short time later I was passing by, and Ho-Jo asked me to slow down and pull in for a cup of coffee. We introduced ourselves and liked each other right away. Then Ho-Jo said, "Paint me." I said I couldn't right away because I was working on an old schoolbus-turned-diner. Ho-Jo was patient. Painting finished, I started thinking about beginnings— Ho-Jo beginnings.

It's 1925, a twenty-seven-year-old man named Howard Deering Johnson was feeling the pain of his father's death; he had to assume all the business obligations, plus going into debt from a small loan. This was in his father's patent medicine store in Quincy, Massachusetts. The soda fountain and newsstand were losing money, and Howard Johnson's misfortune soon started his fortune. The beginning.

The store sold the usual vanilla, chocolate, and strawberry flavors of ice cream, and Howard wanted to sell more flavors. He doubled the butterfat content of his product, added natural ingredients, and perseverance, and came up with a quality ice cream. Customers stood in line for the fourth, fifth, and sixth flavors. With more demand, he was soon selling his ice cream to nearby beaches and other hot spots that wanted cold ice cream.

He opened a little store selling franks and burgers and other prepared foods. He got out of debt, and in 1929 opened another restaurant. At this time he had vision: he knew the roads were going to improve and there would be a need for many roadside restaurants. Then the stock market crashed and his plans changed. Howard Johnson realized that his name was a marque for quality eats, and he offered a few restaurant operators the opportunity to use his name for a fee, providing they would sell his products. This was another beginning: the franchise idea. By 1935 there were twenty-five Howard Johnson's in Massachusetts, and by 1940 there were more than a hundred restaurants along the Atlantic Coast from Massachusetts to Florida. The beginning of the chain.

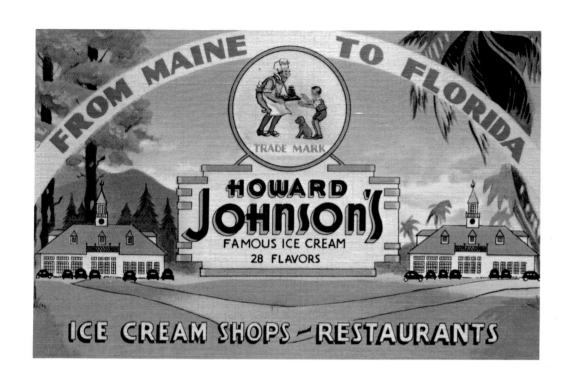

HOWARD JOHNSON'S. ORLEANS. CAPE COD. MASS.

NORTHWAY HOTEL ON CRYSTAL LAKE, BEULAH, MICHIGAN

The exact same Olds.

When I was a kid, a favorite Saturday activity was for my mom to drive "downtown" to visit my dad at "work." My sister Margot and I would pile into the car that I loved so much because I felt so secure in my own little world by myself in the back seat. (I knew that car inside out: it was a 1941 Oldsmobile four-door fastback sedan, navy blue with white side-wall tires on both sides.) I could feel the anticipation growing between me and my sister—a fun-filled day looking at all the shoppers and shopping ourselves, and getting mounds of candy from my dad's sweet-toothed employees.

There were two highlights that made the day for me. One was the odor of roasting coffee as we made our approach to a parking lot. The best was a visual: a giant iceberg that sat on a corner; it was a gas station. I believe it was a Pure Oil Company. On all the trips I would ask my mom to stay in the right lane and to slow down so I could get a respectable glimpse. I would always hope the light was red so I could get a closer look. At times I would ask her to drive in and stop, and she'd say, "But dear, I don't buy my gas there." My conservative mother; I didn't care where she got gas, I needed the experience. A few years later and a little more grown, I noticed that the station was torn down, and I had one of my first experiences of separation anxiety—my first gas station affair.

When my mom did her weekly fill-up, I was always obsessed by the choreography of the "attendant." (In those days one's car was actually attended to.) From the same back seat I would watch with glee. The ritual.

We were "regulars," and the gas-gang knew my mom. They knew her sweet, loving smile and her twinkly, bright blue eyes, and I knew those greasers loved her for her softness—what a break for them. She would greet them with gentility and politeness: "Hello, would you please fill the tank. Thank you." None of that crass "fill-'er-up" stuff. I'd watch the gas pump ritual—the turn of the crank to get the motor running, the gleam of the nozzle, the little orange bulb, all the colors and the sounds, and, oh . . . the odor of the gasoline. My mom would always use "Ethyl," the premium grade; she wanted to feed the Olds a better drink so it would stay new. The odor refreshed my insides; it must have been an early drug experience for me. Then came the windshield wiping. Swish, swish. Slash, slash. Those tough oil-lined hands on a delicate cloth. I'd watch intently the rag pressed to the window. It was like getting my face washed without having to go through the torture. Up went the hood, and all the little secrets of machinery I couldn't figure out—they got their attention. I would see a head disappear and then come up for air. The car got another feeding. Clunk went the hood; it was so long and ungraceful when up, and so long and comfortable when down. The sound of its thud made me shudder; I didn't want it hurt.

My mom would start up, and I'd watch her legs depress the clutch and her arms change gears. I didn't think she should be doing so much work. And we'd drive off, another trip to her regular "Standard" station. I'd look back and see who was next to get the treatment. Then home, and I'd live out the entire experience with my toy cars and gas station. This was my own self-lubrication.

All of us can dig back and feel those tender childhood moments. Those impressions, from the roasted coffee to the iceberg to my "play" garage—they never left me. They just decided to "lodge" themselves in my close friend, the unconscious. They didn't know how long they were going to stay, and neither did I. But, they were content knowing someday I would come back and say hello, and thank those feelings. Those feelings became archetypal images that led me closer to myself and the world around me. Something as minute as pictures of gas stations, and roadside stands, and a row of tourist cabins did that. In a special way, they have served me like an education, and now I wish to share that education—not profess, but share my feelings. Visual feelings.

Arrived in South CaroLina 11:15 AM. Sunday July 5, 1953

South of Border Drive-In-Restaurant Located on Tobacco Trail (U.S. 301) on the North and South CaroLina Border

Cheesberger
Contelope
Coffee

7/5/53 South
11:00 A.M. Lunch
$ 3.50

7/10/53 North
10:00 PM Lunch
1.00

Hot Dogs
Coffee

Hot Dogs
30¢

Bought
Ash Tray

SOUTH OF THE BORDER

LOCATED ON U. S. HIGHWAY
301 & 501 AT S. C. & N. C.
STATE LINE
7 MILES NORTH OF
DILLON, S. C.

OPEN 24 HOURS

SOUTH OF THE BORDER

RESTAURANT & GIFT SHOP

SERVICE STATION ADJOINING

Seven Miles North Of Dillon, S. C., On U. S. Highway 301
On N. C. & S. C. State Line

FINEST IN FOODS & DRINKS

SHELL PETROLEUM PRODUCTS

South of the Border

Leah Schnall, lender of an early "Howard Johnson" postcard ("From Maine To Florida . . .) is a lively, bouncy lady who is el-presidento of the Metropolitan Post Card Club of New York. Leah goes to Florida every year with friends, and like thousands of others stops at motels along the way. Leah has her favorite. We had an emotional discussion about this special place.

"I've been going to the 'South of the Border' every year for about eight, ten years. I always drive straight through. Then, about a hundred miles before you get there, there are signs. Signs all over the place. Huge signs. [higher octave] It's incredible. I get so excited when we get closer. I can hardly wait. I love it there. I won't stay anywhere else. [higher octave] I *love* it. [higher octave] All those Mexican gifts made in Japan. I love it!"

Many people have been telling me about "South of the Border" for years. I scrunch back feeling like a sheltered child and meekly say I never got a chance to get there. I tell Leah about my plight, hoping I will have an understanding soul that will listen and be appreciative of my motel lag.

Leah has known for years that I am a motel freak, at least motels on postcards. There's a high drama approaching; she screams at me.

"Whad'ya mean *you've* never been there!!?!! Of *all* people! You've *never* been there?!? What'sa matter with you?"

Calmed down, Leah says, "I don't believe you've never been there."

Time passes and I see Leah at another postcard wing-ding. I am wearing a putrid chartreuse shirt with "South of the Border" embroidered on the back, "John" embroidered above the front pocket. As Leah is being grossly overwhelmed by my fashion visual, I am being overwhelmed as she is handing me another of the same "Howard Johnson" card, telling me she located one for my personal collection. Elation sets in.

I pay her for the card, and Leah then says, "You *still* haven't been to 'South of the Border'?"

Quaker State

CLARK'S SUPER SERVICE STATION, MERCER, PA.

ON STATE ROUTES #19, #58, #65.—WEST END, COURTHOUSE SQUARE

123139

June, 1981

Jim Michael of Grove City, Pennsylvania, now owns the Quaker State gas station on the courthouse square in Mercer, Pennsylvania. When we met, he was getting ready for the grand opening and was good enough to extend an invitation my way. That was nice, and I would have loved to attend; I've never been to an opening of a gas station, especially one that is approximately sixty years old.

Yes, it was the same station pictured on the card I showed Jim. Jim was surprised to see the postcard (circa 1925), and he was even more surprised when I explained to him it was the same station pictured on the card. The building had gone through its share of embellishments through the years; however, it remained very much intact. I went around the station showing Jim the similarity of architectural detail, right down to the brickwork in the back of the station where no hands had attempted to mask its original identity.

About the time we were making our exit, Jim's attractive wife Ginger pulled in. She had some slight air-conditioning problems in her car, and Jim was attempting to cure the mechanical ills. Ginger was amazed and amused to see the postcard of the station in its earlier days. We talked about the book idea, Cadillacs, the South, and the Grand Ole Opry. They wanted to come to Nashville someday, and we asked them to come see us, "ya hear?"

MEMBERS

UNITED

EASTERN DIV.

MOTOR COURTS

INCORPORATED

INDIVIDUALLY OWNED

FOLLOW THE WHEEL

Free Guide--- Take It

1940 Edition

Corbin, Ky.—MEREDITH'S TOURIST INN. 400 Laurel Ave. on U. S. 25-W. Furnace heat, air-cooled, private baths, inner-spring mattresses; 24-hour service. Phone 248.
J. A. Meredith, Owner-Manager.

Elizabethtown, Ky.—BURNETT'S HOTEL AND MODERN TOURIST COURT. At No. City limits U. S. 31-W. Steam heat, private tub and shower baths, garages. Beautyrest mattresses, playgrounds, swimming pool, cafe. Hayes Burnett, Prop.

Elizabethtown, Ky.—HAYS TOURIST COURT. At No. City limits, on U. S. 31-W. Telephone 3141. (48 Mi. So. of Louisville, Ky.) Telephone and telegraph service. Insulated cottages; steam heat, private tub or shower, inner-spring mattresses, two kitchenettes, car shelter.
Mr. and Mrs. Will H. Hays, Managers & Owners.

Glasgow, Ky.—DUTCH MILL VILLAGE. U. S. 31-E. 30 Mi. East of Bowling Green, 85 Mi. No. of Nashville. Gas heat, private baths, inner-spring beds, grocery, lunch room.
Carroll W. Ream.

Clayton, Ind.—HILLANDALE TOURIST LODGES. So. limits of Indianapolis on U. S. 31, 4402 Madison Ave. Ten minutes to heart of City. Private tiled showers. Year around comfort. Adjacent swimming pool. Phone Drexel 7122.
Noble B. Watson, Owner.

Bardstown, Ky.—WILSON'S TOURIST COURT. In the City, 5 blocks north of the Public Square, on No. 3d St. and U. S. Highways 31-E and 150. White stucco cottages, quiet, attractive surroundings, inner-spring mattresses, private baths, steam heat, garages, personal service. Phone 153.
Mr. and Mrs. A. C. Wilson, Mgr. and Owners.

Bowling Green, Ky.—LOG CABIN COURT. U. S. 31-W, 3 Mi. South, at Lost River. Baths, groceries, lunch room, gas station, closed garages. Mr. and Mrs. G. W. Harwood.

Cave City, Ky.—WIGWAM VILLAGE NO. 2. U. S. 31-W and 68. One Mi. No. of Cave City, 3 Mi. So. of Horse Cave, 11 Mi. East of Mammoth Cave. Baths, fans, heat, inner-springs, spacious grounds, lunch room and gas station, always open. Western Union. Phone 139. F. A. Redford, Owner & Mgr.

Pure Village Cottages

The "Pure Village Cottages" are now named "Village Inn." The name "Pure Village" came directly from the Pure Oil Company, which owned the gas pumps (now gone) and requested the use of their name and architectural motif, better known as the "English Cottage" style. This motif was designed in 1925 exclusively for the Pure Oil Company to overcome resistance to locating stations in residential areas. Oil companies were pressured into making efforts to blend in with neighborhoods, and the cottage motif was a perfect balance for a motel-gas station operator who decided to lease from Pure; thus: "Pure Village Cottages."

Today, one can still observe Pure's sweeping gable and blue tile roof, tall chimneys, bay window, and flower boxes. No more Pure Oil Company, but these fifty-year-old stations are around, some with more make-up and face-lifts than others. The "Village Inn" has added more units, and filled the gaps with more cottages.

O. K. Early opened the "Pure Village Cottages" in 1937, and before that he opened the "Valley Lee" motel, and they sold Shell Oil products, and before that he opened the "Green Lantern" cabins, and they sold Gulf products. I had a chance for a brief chat with O. K.'s son Kermit. He began working for his father after the war in 1946 at the "Pure Village." He was quite familiar with the color card (they gave them away to all their customers), but when I showed him the photocard he said he had never seen it before. Odd. He was a bit preoccupied with some floor moulding, and a customer, and a group of reunion-type men who had just arrived. Kermit has a congenial son, Kevin, who is nineteen and was manning the front desk. Kevin, is studying hotel and restaurant management, and someday he will take the reins of the "Village Inn."

PURE VILLAGE COTTAGES, PHONE 935-L ON US ROUTE 11, 5 MILES S. OF HARRISONBURG VA.

SOUTH EASTERN STATES

PURE OIL
Pathfinder

THE PURE OIL
PURE
COMPANY, U.S.A.

COMPLIMENTS OF
THE SEABOARD OIL COMPANY
Distributors of Pure Oil Products
General Office: Jacksonville, Fla.

THIRTEENTH EDITION

SANDERS COURT
TILE BATHS   STEAM HEAT

SANDERS COURT & CAFE
CORBIN ——— KENTUCKY

Another "Pure" enterprise- this one belonged to the "Colonel," and it's here that "finger-lickin'-good" was created.

THE WINDHAM GRILL — WILLIMANTIC, CONNECTICUT

5A-H1985

HAAG'S WASHINGTON HOUSE

ROOMS -- PRIVATE BATHS -- MEALS
Chicken and Waffle Dinners a Specialty
Phone: 900-8-R-31 Bernville
Sunday Dinners 11 to 7, private tables

4A-H1254

SHARTLESVILLE, PA. -- On Route 22

Haag House

John Setizeninger owns and operates the "Haag House."
He and his family have been there a long, long time. He's
fourth generation. His six sons and two daughters will
probably stick around for a while, too. The original
inn burned down in 1914; the present structure has been
around since 1915.

John and I had a cup of coffee at the bar. Anyone who
loves bars, fine old bars, must get to the "Haag
House" as soon as possible. No adjectives or any exag-
gerations are needed. This pristine vintage bar with
its illustrative stained glass and stick furniture is an
interior experience. Go there. Eat there. Stay in the
inn there. And talk to John Setizeninger.

When I showed John the card, he was very familiar
with it. The inn has been through its share of cards. He
fumbles around under the bar, excuses himself, goes
to the back, and returns with some more cards in his hands.
First is an early sepia photocard; an early twenties
color card with a funny red roof (John said the roof was
never red.); a later black-and-white halftone printed
card with green tinted trees; and then variations of the
late-thirties card that is illustrated.

I keep sipping my coffee and take a closer look at the
sepia photocard. John takes me over to the front
corner by the clock. Under this handsome timepiece is
another segment of the past. Another moment stopped.
There was the original photo that was used for the sepia
postcard. In the picture is his grandfather, A. J. Haag,
with friends in a 1907 Maxwell, and other friends
gathered around the car. Seated in the back of the car is
a gentleman that is his wife's grandfather. Small world.
He asked me to look up from the picture; next to the clock,
attached to the wall, was the original license plate
that was on the car in the photograph.

I asked about the "Dutch Diner," which was a couple of
blocks up the street. (I didn't tell John the significance
the "Dutch Diner" had in shaping a new career and life for
me; that would be getting off base.)

"When I was a kid—oh, around eight or so—I used to go
up to the diner and play pinball–baseball. I did that a
lot for years. I won a lot of free games. And when my
Dad would close up, we'd go up there to grab a bite to eat.
You get tired of eating your own food. . . ."

June, 1981

Lackawanna Trail Diner

Driving back from a bus-nut meet in Hazelton, Pennsylvania, a few years ago, I had the need to visit "Besecker's Diner" on Route 611 in Stroudsburg, Pennsylvania. The purpose was twofold: one, I had an old postcard of "The Lackawanna Trail" diner and knew the original diner was still alive and kicking, and I was curious as to its "remains"; two, I wanted to paint the "remains" of this early O'Mahony dining car. Upon arrival, I saw that it had only a shingle skirt; otherwise, it was intact.

At the time of this writing, July 1981, Robert and Phyllis Besecker, the past owners, have moved on to a larger diner in Stroudsburg. Phyllis told me that the new owners of the old diner have re-named it "The Lackawanna Trail" diner. Yay! (If it were me, I'd restore it exactly like the postcard. Wouldn't you?)

The Besecker family are steeped in diner tradition in the Sullivan county area. Brothers and cousins were all in the diner business. Phyllis's father, Clinton, was telling me about the days he did the "12-12" shift, and the ninety-hour twelve-dollar week. That was 1933-34. "Yup, you could get two doughnuts and all the coffee you want to drink for a nickel. Roast beef, pie, and coffee, for fifty cents. . . . Old Route 611 used to be called the Sullivan Trail, and then it was renamed the Lackawanna Trail. . . . Yeah, there was another diner there in 1923, and then in 1927 'The Lackawanna Trail' was shipped from back east. Yup. Do you know at one time we served near-beer, and the diner was nicknamed, 'The Marble Lounge.' You know—because of the marble counter and tables." Clinton continued, "The new owners of the 'Lackawanna Trail,' well, they have that old postcard you're talking about. They have lots of them. . . ."

D-627

THE LACKAWANNA DINER, ON LACKAWANNA TRAIL, STROUDSBURG, PA.

Oct., 1979

June 1981

Tri-Lakes, Ind.

On the road researching *Gas, Food, and Lodging*, and after feasting on beer and shrimp in Tri-Lakes, Indiana, I experienced another meal that filled me up for a long time.

About fifty feet from the restaurant, which was on one of the Tri-Lakes, there were three of the cutest, coziest, log cabin tourist cabins. I had seen them before—in postcards. I got out the handy picture-taking tool and snapped away, thanking the beautiful early June evening light. Yumm.

While at f.4, a man approached me from the rear.

"What you takin' pictures for?"

Rather than a direct answer, I turned and introduced myself to a kind-looking gentleman. We shook hands firmly, and I met H. J. Everts—white mopped, soft-spoken, with tiny hazel eyes. He was a wrinkleless eighty-two years old.

I told H. J. (Harrison Johns) about *Gas, Food, and Lodging* and my love for old tourist cabins. His hazels

opened wide and he said, "If you have a few moments, I'll tell you about traveling back then." Naturally I knew when *back then* was. I excused myself from my friends. This was to be private, knowing there was a larger feast ahead. We sat down on the grass like two ten-year-olds, cross-legged and ready to share "secret-club" stories.

H. J. filled me in on a little I knew, and a lot I didn't know.

"I did a lot of motor-camping way before there were any tourist-type cabins like those over there. This was around '23 and I was rarin' to get up and go. We were vagabonds then—anyone who had a car. And I was lucky, because I worked damned hard for mine.

There was fellowship on the road, all types of people we'd meet. They were wonderful—from all walks of life. I made some swell friends. We all made our tents, and cooked, and relaxed. I felt like a pioneer; we were all neighbors. Now, let me tell you, the roads, they were awful muddy when it rained. You seen them in pictures, but it

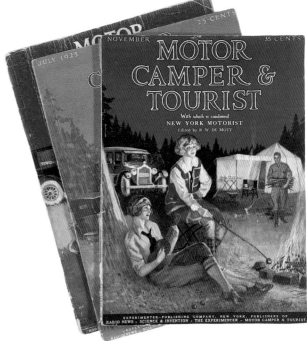

was worse. Ah, you've never experienced that mess, have you? You young folks, so spoilt. You know that?" (I nodded.)

I told H. J. that I knew motor-camping was a national pastime, and that I had read a lot of material on the hobby. I had become acquainted with it through my postcards, a number of articles, and about a dozen issues of *Motor Camper & Tourist*, which was loaded with articles and pictures of the period. He remembered the magazine and knew one of the writers. I asked him if he remembered such terms as "Motor-Hoboing" and "Tin-Canners" and other lower-echelon names that applied to motor-campers. He did, of course, and we talked a little about the darker elements, and the true gypsies of the road that wandered from camp to camp and how they hurt the business.

Quickly I excused myself from H. J. and ran to the car, and ran back with a manila folder laden with motor-camping and tourist cabin postcards. His face looked surprised, and the hazels got larger again. "Where did you get these?" H. J. asks, and I told him they were part of many years of collecting. He smiled, and I could see a little devil in his eyes. He started to tell me about a romance that was started at a campsite. It got wonderfully funny,

risque, and contemporary. That was a perfect bridge for my next question.

With fluttering "Groucho" eyebrows, I asked H. J. about cottage life—the so-called "transition" period from campsites to sheltered quarters. I told him I read that part of the cottage business was called "bounce-on-the-bed" trade. He read me, and replied, "No, no, no . . . I wasn't like that. I raised some hell, but none of that stuff." H. J. is now smiling from one earlobe to the other, and we both look over to the little log cabin cottages.

"I got married to my Nell in 1927. Now, we didn't have time to hanky-panky."

I asked, "What were you doing then?"

"Oh, I was an industrial engineer. My father was, too, one of the first. My son, too. How about that?"

Not wanting to get too much into family matters, I asked about his grandson and if he was an aspiring engineer. "Aspiring, hell, he's a professor of I. E. at Cal-Tech. How about that? . . . How did you know I had a grandson?"

I knew. "I just knew; you look like a grandfather."

"Yep, I have five grandchildren. The rest are beautiful girls."

Shady Rest

"Shady Rest" is probably one of the more popular names affixed to tourist cabins and motels. Obvious idea. I always wanted to visit a "Shady Rest" and see what it was all about.

Route 40 to and from Zanesville, Ohio, was a major route prior to the interstate highway. A Travel Lodge owner and native of Zanesville told me that the structure behind the gas station on the card was presently someone's home. Off we go looking for the remains of the "Shady Rest."

I can't find it, even with proper directions. It's raining and that adds confusion. Where *was* the place? Where's the "Shade"? On one of the drive-bys we were attracted to a group of miniature, painted holstein cows standing on a lawn close to the road. Just like in real life. They looked like midget holsteins. Instead they were contemporary roadside folk art. Another roadside attraction, and invitation. Up the gravel we go and into a garage and into a little office-flea-market. We meet George Buchanan, a receptive, burly, highly enthusiastic real estate developer, builder, carpet dealer, furniture dealer, high-roller, and county commissioner. I show him the card of the "Shady Rest Tourist Court." "Yes-siree I *sure* do remember that place. It's right down the road at the corner of Jackson, not far, just down the road [I'm really feeling out of it here, after missing it twice.] . . . glad to see this." He directs us again with more formality.

George shows the card to his son. It's his twenty-first birthday, and he's already built his fifth house. His son seemed to care less, but George was getting hot. He started to call a few people. He's on the phone with a friend, "Hey, Tom, you remember the old service station, the Sohio one, it had the cabins at the back. . . . You probably shacked up there when you were a kid. . . ." I'm listening intently and at the same time thumbing through a boxful of motel cards. Jane is eyeballing a beautiful cobalt biscuit jar. George is on another call, ". . . the log-cabin; yeah, it was a restaurant; yeah, it had dopies in it for a while, and they tore it down recently. . . ." He talks some more about his business, and traveling, and spontaneous trips he takes with his wife, and his multiple businesses, and we decide the holsteins are too expensive to ship. And George makes another call; he's still hot.

Shady Rest Tourist Camp, Modern Cabins.
3 Miles East of Zanesville, Ohio. On Route 40.

June, 1981

"Hello, Dave, there's some people here that want to know about the old gas station and cabins down the road. Your step-granddaddy owned it for a while, didn't he? . . . They are going to come over and see you. . . ."

George takes another good look at the card. He's smiling. There are stories on his face. "This was the big-gee here. Been there hundreds of times. Hmmmmm, the old Shady Rest. That's where it got its name—the trees up there. See 'em?"

It was difficult leaving George. We could have stayed on for a while just talking away. George has a lust for life and business that's rare today; it comes from his inside and you feel it. His friendship and warmth was like a warm blanket that covered us on that cold and rainy day.

George's friend Dave remembered the gas station in a focused and intimate way. When he was a kid in the forties, he and his older brother didn't have the luxury of visiting their step-grandfather, so they would jaunt down to the gas station and hang around and chew bubble gum. Being brand-oriented, and recalling only one decent bubble gum of the day, I asked Dave if it was "Fleer's Double-Bubble." He nodded with a twinkle in his eye.

Back down to reinvestigate the "Shady-Rest" and take some pics. It has suffered the pangs of time. The house is there, and hardly recognizable. The front gable gives it away at a second glance. Everything else is gone. The cabins have been replaced by mobile homes.

109

The Diamonds

I was looking at a few of "The Diamonds" cards, which aren't particularly attractive, and said to myself, "Hey, what is this 'largest roadside restaurant' business?" I knew there was more to this story; I just felt it oozing out of the printing ink, and the aerial photo. I knew these kinds of operations come and go, and, knowing I didn't have time to make a trip to Missouri, I picked up the phone.

Jack Echelkamp is on the line—he's the assistant manager. Jack is now fifty-seven and started working at "The Diamonds" when he was fifteen. "I worked my way up, yes, sir, and I'm still trying to get to the top, too. It's a long climb. My brother-in-law is the manager. I'll have to wait 'til he leaves. . . ."

"What about this 'largest' idea, Jack?"

"Well, you see, this is an unincorporated area. There are places in big cities that may be largest, but this is an unincorporated area. It's the largest, yes."

"How did the 'largest roadside restaurant' get started? Who was behind it? I mean, Jack, it looks like the kind of place that started with nothing and grew and grew and grew."

"OK, if you got a few minutes, I'll tell you. . . .

"First of all, you're right, it grew leaps and bounds. A character by the name of Spencer Groff owned it—he was a lawyer, and had bad times. You know, he lost a lot of dough, and he had to pay off his business failures. He was past forty, and, back then (the early twenties), at that age most people were pretty much on top of their life. Well, one day, as the story goes, he was standing on the road at a fork, and watching all the people go by in their cars. He knew all these people were customers for something. So, one Labor Day he figured he'd stop a lot of these travelers going home and sell them some plums that were picked from across the road. Along with the plums he had a tub full of soda pop. That's how he began."

"And what happened after that, did he build a stand?"

"Nope, what happened was he didn't do anything until the next summer.

"He took a top from a silo, and used it for a roof, and he put up a railing, and sold more fruits and drinks. He didn't want to go through another year of closing, so he enclosed the stand and put up a gas pump so he could get some extra business in the colder months. He served hot dogs and cold buttermilk and melons and fruit and fresh vegetables and work clothes."

"When was this?" I said.

"I guess it was around the mid-twenties. His business was booming, just mushroomed, and he needed a larger place. At the same fork in the road where he started a few years back, at the same corner, he drew an outline on the ground that was in the shape of a baseball diamond. He built a building in the shape of a diamond."

I said, "I bet it was white clapboard and called 'The Diamond.'"

"Wait, you're half right. It was white clapboard, but it was called 'The Banana Stand,' and he had bunches of bananas painted all over it. It stayed open all night; he never closed it. Business got bigger and better and he built another 'Banana Stand,' and a storm came along right after it was built and it was torn down to the ground. Mr. Groff picked himself up and built another place, but this time he called it 'The Diamonds'—that was in 1927. Yeah, he had some bad times. But, he was a religious man and he pulled through many a tough situation."

I asked, "What does it look like now?"

"It's not the one on the postcard you're looking at. We're in a different place. The old one stood vacant from 1969 to 1972, which is when we moved two miles east. The old place is now a truck stop. Yes, sir, ol' Mr. Groff; too bad, he wanted his money to go to a Baptist orphanage, but that never happened."

I thanked Jack for all the information.

"I'll send you a new card. It's got the old sign—you'll like that, and, if you can spare a couple of bucks, I'll send you a book that's a story of Spencer Groff. Now, I'll tell you, it's old—goes back to 1936."

Again I thanked Jack for a great telephone trip. I put a couple of dollars in the mail, and a week later I was digging into *Diamond Dust*.

WORLD'S LARGEST ROADSIDE RESTAURANT

The DIAMONDS
RESTAURANT
**25 MODERN
TOURIST COTTAGES**
AT JUNCTION
U. S. 66 - U. S. 50
MO. 100
P.O. VILLA RIDGE, MO.

SERVING OVER
1,000,000 CUSTOMERS A YEAR

NOVELTY AND CAFETERIA
SERVING AREA ▷

◁ DINING AREA AND
QUICK LUNCH FOUNTAIN

PHONES

OUR COFFEE
IS SO
GOOD
We always drink it *Ourselves!*

THE DIAMONDS RESTAURANT AND CABINS

JUNCTION 50-66-100   VILLA RIDGE, MO.

Geyer's

"Geyer's" still stands. No more pumps, but cabins in the backyard. About three of them. "Geyer's" is now "Goody's" restaurant. It was closed the day I visited there, but I spoke with a pleasant man who had been around Shippensburg for a while. His name is Frank Haller, and Frank has had the local Cadillac, Oldsmobile, and Chevrolet dealership there since 1932.

Frank looked at the card. He had never seen it before, but he knew the photographer. He said he was the leading local photographer for a forty-year period. He had gone to school with his daughter, and later sold her a car.

"What kind of pictures did he take, Frank?"

"He took scenes. The teachers college. Kids pictures. Buildings. . . . I'm *very* surprised to see he did advertising pictures."

June, 1981

GEYER'S CABIN CAMP
HEATED CABINS
HOT SHOWERS
KITCHEN AND LAUNDRY

COMPLETE LINE OF GROCERIES
GAS AND OIL
GARAGE SERVICE

BELL PHONE 9036 H.W. GEYER PROP. SHIPPENSBURG, PA. U.S. ROUTE 11.

112

Little Cabin Inn

In 1923, Rose Mazoll Magyr and her mother and father started a fruit stand and a two-pump Tydol gas station (later Mobil and then Esso). In 1934, Rose married, and her new husband joined the family business. By that time they had built a restaurant and lunchroom, and had cabins a quarter of a mile up the then-new Route 9W, north of Newburgh, New York. The "Little Cabin Inn" is not a postcard. It *should* be. The photo was taken in May, 1981. When I drove by the "Little Cabin Inn," I knew I was in a time warp and was driving *by* a postcard. It felt good, a life-size postcard in three dimensions. Little did I know I would soon be entering the fourth. I decided to keep cool and hold my excitement down. I swung around, and had the tank filled up while asking questions of Rose's son, Junior. He began to tell me a brief story about how his mother started the place. I began to drool. I then pulled out a "dummy" of *Gas, Food, and Lodging.* He began to understand and appreciate my interest, and concerns. He went to get his mother, and within seconds we all were sitting at a table in the old lunchroom.

I began to tell Rose of my quest, the yearning to go back to places on postcards that had anything to do with gas, food, or lodging. She was delighted that I had paid attention to her old station. I told them how rare it was to see someone who still cares to keep it the way it "was." Rose proceeded to tell me she was an old-fashioned person and wanted to keep things the "old way." She used to serve over 300 meals a day, and during World War II more than eighty weddings took place there. They stopped serving food in 1974; however, through a door in the restaurant is a bar that still is operative. It is beautiful and completely wood paneled—intact from day one, but Rose apologized for its need to be cleaned. It didn't seem time had made any mark on it.

She brought out a scrapbook that hadn't been opened in many years, and Junior casually joined us. My feelings were as though I had opened a piece of the past that hadn't been dealt with for a long time. I began to take notice of Rose. Her character and name meshed perfectly: like a rose, she was calm and graceful. Soft and quiet. Old fashioned and intact. We sifted through the pictures: Junior as a little boy, her husband in the classic stance next to the gas pump, the family in the backyard. I was asking questions, and often they were going over her head. She was totally immersed in the scrapbook. She was touched. I was touched.

I asked whether she had any old postcards. Rose told me they used to give them away. They had black-and-whites and color, but only of the cabins. None of the station. I began to wonder if one had ever passed my way, and in my vast collection was there a "Little Cabin Inn" postcard lurking around somewhere?

And then we had an uncanny connection. I told her I knew Magyr was a Hungarian name. (In fact it literally means "Hungarian.") She told me her husband had come from Budapest. I told her my father had come from Budapest. I asked how Junior got his name. "Well, when he was a little boy, he didn't like Julius, and all his friends didn't like Julius, so we called him Junior, and the name has been with him ever since." So I asked Junior the name of his three-year-old son. He said it was Joseph. Already feeling rich from the past half hour of talk, I told them my father's first two names were Julius Joseph.

May, 1981

HIDDEN INN

YOU ARE NOW AT
HIDDEN INN
DINNERS   CABINS

LAKESIDE
INN

DU-KUM-IN.   4TH LAKE.

"Turn Inn"
Tourists
Falmouth Foreside - Portland, Me.
3 Miles East of Portland - Route 1
1/8 Mile from Marine Hospital
PhoNE 3 - 2138

ICE DREAM PARLORS.

DU-KUM-IN

TURN INN

THIS WAS OUR CABIN

Good Luck Inn, on Roosevelt Highway, near Towanda, Pa.

SWING INN - CABINS, U.S. 41, 3 M. NO. TURKEY RUN STATE PARK, P.O. BLOOMINGDALE, IND.

Travelers' Inn 13 miles west of Hancock, Md. U.S. 40

Nettland's Roll Inn on Highway 16 "At the Dells" Wisconsin Dells, Wis. 1-31.

Main St., Mosinee, Wis.   R-26

The sacred small town.

The "road" postcard was used basically for advertising and promotion: the friendly reminder to "come back and see us, ya hear," or the souvenir for the daily record that may end up in a scrapbook or a top drawer for several years—the little, ephemeral pictorial communicator to send a friend or loved one. It is a universal experience we have all shared. (*Who* hasn't written or received a postcard?)

But what about the "town" postcard—the *small* town that was between the vast stretches of road, the small town sitting quietly with all its secrets, the small town that is connected to its heart—*the* pulse of its own place, personally historic and secure within generations. The small town that gave gas, food, and lodging to those who wanted to get off the road and go from one linear experience to another. This involvement was on the streets, and the linear experience was going from establishment to establishment. Different needs being met, but the same basics working.

Small towns are the fiber that makes up the weave of the American character. I love small towns. I love small-town postcards. In postcard circles, photocards of small towns are called "local views." The local view card is an umbrella for many interests: the main street; the town itself that belongs to a specific state; a particular commercial building (bank, post office, drug store, theater, hotel, etc.); and for some of us the beauty of a particular make of car(s). I personally am drawn to people walking across a street—the gesture caught by the camera, time caught against the "backdrop" of the townscape.

I consider these photocards the most unique and extensive visual record of our cherished past. I feel that the photographers who were responsible for thousands of these *views*—all unknowns, all humble servants, all masters of their trade—made a definite mark on the community with their visual tact and compassion.

MAIN ST., FRIENDSHIP, ME.

Main Street Torrington Wyo.

Main Street Abottsford, Wis. T-212

STREET SCENE EFFINGHAM ILL.

MAIN STREET - GRANGEVILLE, IDAHO.

MAIN ST NORTH MILFORD IA. 4101

Quincy, Mich.

MAIN STREET WEBSTER, WIS.

WALL STREET - EAGLE RIVER, WIS.   Johnson Photo

My '49 Cadillac

Small town postcard scenes offer other rewards. Recently I had a peak experience at a New York Postcard Show, sponsored by Leah Schnall of "South of the Border" fame.

I love old cars, Cadillacs in particular. Cadillac has always been an engineering and style leader, no matter *what* another car nut will tell you. Among a few I own, one is a 1949 two-door "Sedanette," which was the last year of the sleek fastback design that was very popular from 1941 through 1949. They're handsome dressed in black, burgundy, or navy blue, but mine is "El Paso Beige."

I had this intense need to locate a '49, like mine, on a postcard, and hopefully in a small town on a photocard.

Obsession set in, and I was going through *all* my cards. Plenty of Cadillacs, but no '49 two-door. I was disappointed, but wasn't going to give up. The next day I am with postcard dealer Sandy Millns of Toledo, Ohio, rummaging through some gas stations, a few buses, and some small town scenes. Yikes! There it is, my '49 Cadillac, in "El Paso Beige," rounding the corner on Wall Street in Eagle River, Wisconsin.

Who are those people in that car? Where have they been? Where are they going? Whatever happened to them? Whatever happened to the Cadillac? Is it mine *now*?

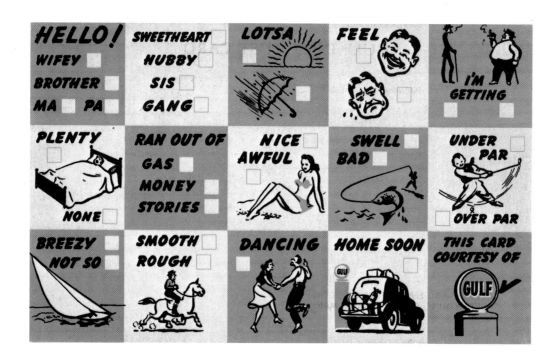

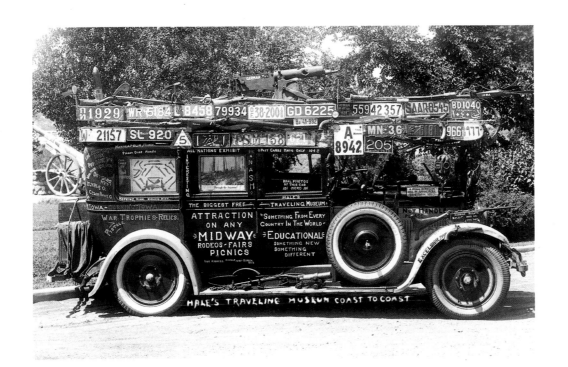

The magic of a few words.

1643
WHITE HORSE SERVICE STATION has twelve
pumps serving five major brands of gasoline, two acres of
excellent parking space and its air of cleanliness always
makes it justly termed Western New York's finest highway station.

Hello—
White Horse + gas
+ choc. bar at 6:15
Silver Creek 6:30
Erie 8:00 fire
Point? ash
10 til 9 everything
OK 10K

Relax and Enjoy Our
Western Hospitality In
Pleasant Surroundings
GERRY'S CAFE
Bob's Mobil Service in Conjunction.

Hi Folks:
Arrived Sat. 11 AM
Every one fine. Grandma
tired but Happy— Linda
impressed with scenary—
miss you Both. say Hi
to Cricket— Kids are Having
a ball Brian + Jeff Really
took up with uncle cliff
Jeff still Reluctent with
Aunt Marce—
Love Mel + family

COLONIAL COURT
35 Units
Air-Conditioned — Hot Water Heat
Combination Tile Baths and Showers
Fully Carpeted Floors—Beautyrest Mattresses
Large Lobby and Office
South Main on U. S. 41 — Tel. 96
"Madisonville's Finest"

Dearest Folks,
Beautiful drive today.
So far very good.
Vickie is so excited
about 3 tiny bars of
Palmolive soap + what
she calls a nice little
house. This is a
nice place. Love
Don, Jer + Vic

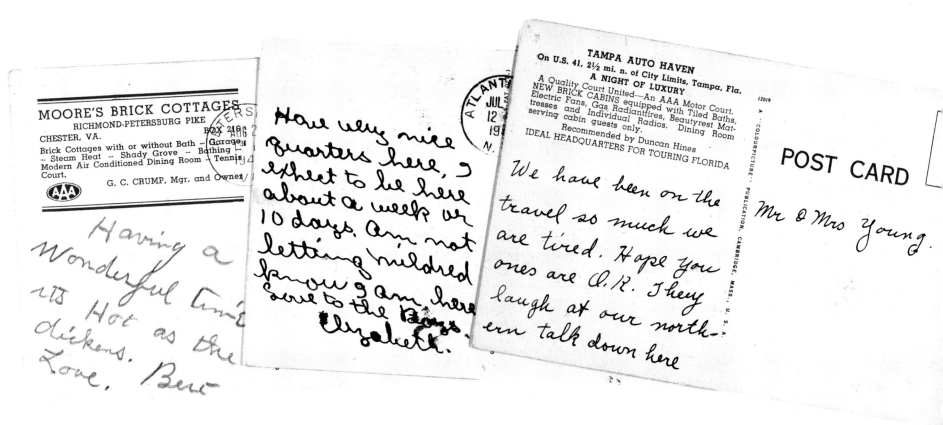

In the postcard market, a used card has less "dollar" value than an unused card. Unused cards—void of any cancellations, postage, or written messages—have a more precious and pristine appearance. They have been less-handled, too. I find the used card of interest for a couple of reasons.

A card that has been "handled" has more life in it. And around it. It has more spirit. (I'm not referring to the creased card with torn corners and yellowed tape from an album . . .) Used cards have a *sense* of the sender. (Like people who have a *sense* of themselves.) Where they've been and where they're going. Mysterious elements. Personal history. Immediacy. Yes, these characteristics are fleeting, and ephemeral, but a used card is locked more into time and space because of the life it has been through, and the life it will carry on.

I find myself involved with memories from a stranger—stepping into his intimate world. Intervening without invitation. The postcards leave their "world" and become open for others to appreciate, love, and share.

Depending on one's style of writing, style of thinking,

style of communication, the space on a postcard back offers little (or a lot) of room for a message. The intrigue about the space and what people allot themselves is fascinating and fun to observe. Few moments are taken to write about a few moments, or a few hours, or a few days. Time is condensed into an area of approximately $2\frac{1}{2}$ x $2\frac{3}{4}$".

There is magic that occurs in this intense area of space. The magic is in the physical space and the time that is communicated in the space. Is this another intellectual study of space–time relationships? Maybe. Maybe not. Let the heavy-headed deal with this.

Some of these messages touch me deeply. They hit tender nerve endings that transcend the visual part of the card. Time becomes more outward and raw. Naked. Time becomes a patina, and this patina is transformed into another form: it becomes poetry. If we examine these simple and yet complex messages, they provide a clue to our heritage, just as the images serve as visual artifact. Not much different from a wall painting in an Egyptian tomb.

These postcards are true icons of our roadside culture.

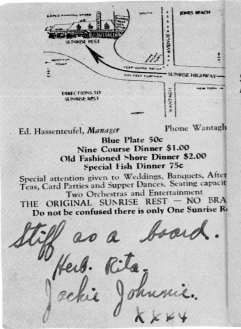

POST CARD

Oct 17-47, Friday 4:45 P.M,
Thought I hate demonse ordock.
and got a ham sandwich Instead.
what a stinging.

POST CARD

Very good looking on a
post card - but not so good
when you are here.

DIRECTIONS TO
SUNRISE REST

Ed. Hassenteufel, *Manager*   Phone Wantagh
Blue Plate 50c
Nine Course Dinner $1.00
Old Fashioned Shore Dinner $2.00
Special Fish Dinner 75c
Special attention given to Weddings, Banquets, After
Teas, Card Parties and Supper Dances. Seating capacit
Two Orchestras and Entertainment
THE ORIGINAL SUNRISE REST — NO BRA
Do not be confused there is only One Sunrise R

Stiff as a board.
Herb. Rita.
Jackie Johnnie.
xxxx

Paddock Diner
Located on Pulaski Hwy., Route
White Marsh, Maryland
Midway between Baltimore and Abe
Serving Home-Cooked Meals and Home-M
AIR-CONDITIONED — TRUCKERS W
Open 24 hours:
Owned and Operated by: Elmer F. S
Telephone: Chase-2883

not much
see on the way
Bet

82837

THE CAROUSEL
Tallahassee's newest and smartest place to eat.
Famous for Sea Food and U.S. choice Meats.
Fountain service - Open 24 hours.
318 N. Monroe St. - Phone 3-0473
Tallahassee, Fla.

RED SAILS INN
"The Sea Food Center"
On Fishermen's Wharf   654 Harbor D
SAN DIEGO, CALIFORNIA
Under the personal supervision
of the proprietors, Mr. & Mrs. Viery
— Telephone: Franklin 2332 —
Located where the book "I Cover the W
front" was written. Justly famous for
delicious six-course Sea Food Dinners at p
lar prices.

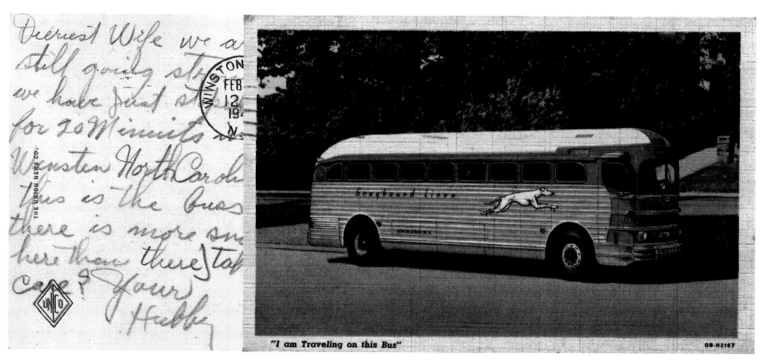

"I am Traveling on this Bus"

OB-H2167

In the lower left margin, note the quote: "I am Traveling on this Bus." The back of this card reads:

> *Dearest Wife we are still going*
> *strong we have just stopped for 20*
> *minutes in Winsten Caroling*
> *there is more snow here than there*
> *take care?*   *Your Hubby*

The card was postmarked February 5, 1944, 12 AM, from Winston-Salem, N.C., and sent to Albany, New York.

I did not cite this message as a mockery of misspelling. This is a poignant note—touching and loving. There were a large majority of people who weren't blessed with the convenience of an automobile. They had to travel long, hard hours by bus, or train. They traveled and toured the roads of America in a less-private and more-communal fashion.

FLAGSHIP 29

Highway 29 UNION, N. J.

★ A nautical spot on New Jersey's Highway 29, seven miles from Newark, best known for its excellent food and drinks at moderate prices. Catering to a host of daily satisfied patrons and banquet parties -- the rendezvous for travelers and sightseers. Dancing to the soft strains of the Flagship Orchestra every evening.

Visit our Famous Compass Bar

GENUINE CURTEICH-CHICAGO "C.T. PHOTO-COLORIT" POSTCARD (REG. U.S. PAT. OFF.)

Hello Junie
How is you.
Received your letter
yesterday [illegible]
[illegible]
Love
Jimmy

PLACE STAMP HERE

POST CARD

A1217

MWM "COLOR-LITHO" MADE ONLY BY MID-WEST MAP CO., AURORA, MO.

Santa Fe, New Mexico
The City Different
HACIENDA COURT
On Highway 85 - One-half Mile from West City Limits - New - Modern in every way

M milk	20
Cards	75
Cards	10
Shoes S	3.00
Bus Fair	2 25
Pictures	4 15
Pictures	2 00
Lunch	50
Lunch	50
Ice C	20
Cards	50
Lunch	1.00
Ice Cream	40
Raido	1 25
Cards	10
Boots	9.00
Mame Pete	5
Sarapy	65

Maria, Look at this beautiful place. Doesn't it remind you of a church in Europe somewhere? It is a really pretty inside with wood on the ceiling and wood all over the walls.

We filled up our gas tanks here and drove for 5 hours straight and rested while eating hamburgers. Nippy the dog got sick from the hamburgers. Say, thank you for sending along the asparagus. See you in a few weeks. Love, Jon,

127

SHELL
MOTOR ROAD GUIDE

INDIANA

Compliments of
Roxana Petroleum Corporation
ST. LOUIS, MISSOURI

CAMEL ROOM — LITTLE OASIS
53rd and Girard Avenue — Philadelphia, Pa.

Williams Restaurant, Buffalo, Mo.

GENE'S GRILL — *Carthage's Popular Eating Place*

Index